Awop Bop Aloo Mop

ALSO BY TINA ANDREWS

PRINCESS SARAH:
Queen Victoria's African Goddaughter

CHARLOTTE SOPHIA:
Myth, Madness and the Moor

SALLY HEMINGS AN AMERICAN SCANDAL:
The Struggle To Tell The Controversial True Story

Awop Bop Aloo Mop

Little Richard:
A Life of
Sex, Drugs, Rock & Roll...

...and Religion

TINA
ANDREWS

The Malibu Press
New York Los Angeles London

The author gratefully acknowledges permission from the
following sources: The New York Times, Rolling Stone
magazine, The Washington Post and British GQ magazine
to reprint excerpts from previously published articles.

Published by The Malibu Press

Logo and colophon are registered trademarks of:

The Malibu Press
954 Lexington Avenue
New York, NY 10021
Email: info@themalibupress.com
Website: www.themalibupress.com

10 9 8 7 6 5 4 3 2 1

Cover and Book Design by
Leigh Kirkwell

ISBN-13: 9780998226064

Library-of-Congress Cataloging-in-Publication Data is available.

Limited Special First Edition

Printed and Manufactured in the United States

Dedicated to:

The one and only Little Richard
The Architect of Rock & Roll
and inspiration of millions

to
Wendy Kram
who always believed

and
My niece Rachel
who carries the torch forward.

*"And there appeared a great
wonder in the sky..."*

Revelation 12:1

*"I saw a great flash of light in the sky.
I took it as a sign I gotta sing God's music"*

Little Richard

Contents

Introduction

"When you're dead and there's dirt on your grave, then they'll say how great you were, but you'll never get to hear it. It's black music. Why won't they just say it? If it's pork, say it comes from the pig. If it's beef, say it comes from the cow. If it's rock & roll, say it comes from black people."

—Little Richard, 1999

T rue story. I was four years old when Little Richard's *Tutti Fruitti* hit the airwaves in 1955. My
parents played that 45 record so much on their little
hand-held record player they went through two copies of the song and two needles had to be replaced.
My mom and dad could really dance. They tore it up
to that record and I loved watching them. I was told
that because I heard the song so often I could be seen
dancing in the long hallway of our Prairie Avenue
southside apartment in Chicago singing:

"*Awopaboppaloobopalopabingbang.*"

Okay. So those weren't the exact words. But you
catch the drift—and the drift was that Rock & Roll
transformed American culture more profoundly than
any other art form.

Yet to understand that art form you must accept
and appreciate its roots—for they are deeply embed-
ded in black culture.

Coming out of Rhythm and Blues, which itself came
out of gospel, blues music was created by black slaves
who adapted their African musical heritage to the
American environment in which they sadly found

themselves. Taking many forms, and undergoing many permutations throughout the years, blues formed the basis of jazz, rhythm and blues, and ultimately rock & roll.

Torn from their kin, enduring a brutal journey from their beloved homes in West Africa to the American South on slave ships, Africans were forced into a servile way of life. They tried to retain some continuity with their past in a variety of ways, including music. Their voices glided between the more rigid European musical scale to create a distinctive new sound.

One observer wrote in 1845, "Our black oarsmen made the woods echo to their songs. One of them, taking the lead, improvised a verse, then others joined in the chorus, always repeating the same words."

Some slaves, especially those from the Bantu tribe, whooped or jumped octaves during the call-and-response, which served as a basis for field hollers.

Slaves, accustomed to dancing and singing to the beat of drums in Africa, emphasized rhythm in their music. In a single song they clapped, danced, and slapped their bodies in myriad different rhythms, compensating for the absence of drums, which were outlawed by plantation owners. These owners feared that the instrument would be used to coordinate slave insurrections. One ex-slave, writing in 1853, called the rhythmic practice "patting juba." It was performed by "striking the right shoulder with one hand—all the while keeping time with the feet and singing."

African Americans used these African musical traits in their religious ceremonies. One writer in the *Nation* described a "praise-meeting" held in 1867: "At regular intervals one hears an elder wailing a hymn sung two lines at a time, and whose wailing cadences into the night air are indescribably melancholy."

The subsequent response from the congregation to the bluesy call of the elder, along with the accompanying instruments, created the call-and-response, the rhythmic complexity, and the minor-key sound common in African music.

Such African-inspired church music, later known as spirituals, became the basis for the blues, when singers applied the religious music to secular themes.

In the early 50s, Richard Wayne Penniman applied these musical principles, sped up the beat, changed the keys from minor to major, and created this new musical genre that everyone worldwide began to embrace...

...Rock & Roll.

The art form incorporated teen angst and the emotions exploding from the lives that informed it. It reflected its surroundings e.g., the need to escape, be free, and to "let off steam." No one had more of an impact on all of it than Little Richard.

Richard Penniman burst onto the American scene in 1955 with *Tutti Fruitti* and almost by himself poured the concrete to cement the anti-rules for this exciting new music. Dubbing himself "The Architect of Rock & Roll," he had the biggest influence on musicians and singers, black and white, with his wild performances which included standing up playing piano—sometimes with a foot up on the keyboard, jumping onto the piano and dancing; and wearing outrageous, androgynous costuming including sequined tuxedo's, glittered shoes and velvet capes, coupled with pancake make-up, eyeliner and a foot-high pompadour hairdo.

He was an scandalous thing to behold.

FLASH FORWARD. I finally got to meet Little Richard in 1998 on the set of my first produced film as a screenwriter, Warner Bros. *"Why Do Fools Fall In Love,"* directed by Gregory Nava *("Selena")*. The film chronicled the life of 1950's teenaged sensation Frankie Lymon who died of a drug overdose at age 25. In it Little Richard played himself in the

Little Richard and Frankie Lymon, 1956. Lymon would succumb to a heroin overdose in 1968.

courtroom scenes for a lawsuit brought against Morris Levy and Roulette Records for royalties owed the Frankie Lymon estate. Later in the film, Richard performed *Keep A'Knockin'* and was sensational. Because Richard had brought on a similar lawsuit with his former label, Specialty Records and its owner Art Rupe, I wanted the real Little Richard to appear in the film to lend gravitas. He and I spent many hours in his dressing room chatting about showbusiness, Rock & Roll and his role in it. He was a fountain of anecdotes and information. Since he knew Frankie, I had to ask him how it felt to lose the young star to heroin addiction the same year as Martin Luther King Jr., and Bobby Kennedy. Since Richard was battling his own addiction in those days, I wondered if Frankie's death portended a future that could have been Richard's own. Using one of his favorite phrases he answered, "It shook my mind."

Well, Little Richard shook mine.

I knew that at some point I would have to tell his story and have been astonished it has taken so long to shine a light on the man who had such a huge impact in the creation of Rock & Roll and the stage personas of so many performers in it. Yes, Ma Rainey and Chuck Berry deserve credit also to some musical purists, but Little Richard and his music can be heard in the sounds and performances of countless legends and everyone we enjoy or have enjoyed from Mick Jagger, to Michael Jackson, to Prince, the Rolling Stones, Paul McCartney, The Beatles, Elvis Presley, James Brown, Jerry Lee Lewis, David Bowie, Lady Gaga and Keith Richards who all cite Richard as their inspiration. The list is endless.

Rolling Stones front man Mick Jagger tells of watching Little Richard perform and being inspired to not only sing and dance but sing and dance *"like that."* He and Keith Richards were profoundly influenced by Little Richard, and Jagger cites him as his introduction to R&B music: *"Nobody could beat Little Richard's stage act. Little Richard is the originator and my first idol."*[1] When Keith Richards heard *Tutti Fruitti* for the first time, he recalls, *"It was as though the world changed suddenly from monochrome to Technicolor."*[2]

Richard was an early vocal influence on Rod Stewart who said, *"I remember trying to sound like Little Richard."*[3] David Bowie called Little Richard his *"inspiration,"* stating that upon listening to *Tutti Frutti that he "heard God."*[4] Then there is Bob Dylan who, when leaving school in 1959, wrote in his high school yearbook under "Ambition": "To join Little Richard."

After opening for Richard with his band Bluesology, pianist Reginald Dwight became enthused. Later changing his name to Elton John, he said: *"When I saw Little Richard standing on top of the piano, all the stage lights, sequins and energy, I decided then and there that I wanted to be a rock and roll piano player."*[5]

Several members of The Beatles (featured in Chapter 10) were also heavily influenced by Richard including Paul McCartney and George Harrison. McCartney idolized him in school and later used his recordings as inspiration for his uptempo rockers such as *I'm Down*. In fact,

Long Tall Sally was the first song McCartney performed in public.[6]

And it continued well into the 80s and 90s. Trust me—there would be no Rick James, Prince, Morris Day or Michael Jackson without Little Richard. Prince has said that his androgynous look, music and vocal style were owed to Little Richard—whose protégé Jimi Hendrix, once a band member, would later say *"...I wanted to do with my guitar what Richard did with his voice."*[7]

Farrokh Bulsara performed many covers of Little Richard's songs as a teenager, before finding fame as Freddie Mercury, the lead singer for Queen.

Even more contemporary performers like Mystikal, André "André 3000" Benjamin of Outkast, and Bruno Mars were cited by critics as having emulated Little Richard's style in their own works. Mystikal's vocal rap delivery was compared to Richard's.[8] André 3000's vocals in Outkast's hit *Hey Ya!* were compared to an *"indie rock Little Richard."*[9] Bruno Mars has admitted Little Richard was one of his earliest influences.[10] Mars' song, *Runaway Baby* from his album, *Doo-Wops & Hooligans* was cited by *The New York Times* as "channeling Little Richard."[11]

On songs like *Tutti-Frutti* and *Lucille,* Richard sounded like a exorcist priest wrestling the devil out of a possessed man. His falsetto screeches eviscerated the rules of pop singing. His was a voice that leapt from a transistor radio and left singe marks on a generation of performers. Additionally, Little Richard altered the consensus in America (and the world) that blacks could only do one kind of music—Race music.

1950s Rock & Roll music, pioneered by black musicians, was racially inclusive and attracted listeners and performers reaching across the color line.

The contemporary view of rock as music made *by* white people *for* white people is shortsighted and, frankly, inaccurate. For me, an African American fan of rock who is accustomed to and tired of the view that rock is music in which black people are not supposed to participate, it became important to write a full-on sketch of the one performer who represents not only the origins of the genre, but the music rendered by a black man, and a black queer man at that.

Somehow, the music Little Richard created was co-opted by whites and became a musical genre called simply "Rock" music in which suddenly black people were rendered inauthentic who performed it.

By the time Jimi Hendrix (featured in Chapter 13) died in 1970, and later when Lenny Kravitz rose to prominence, the idea of a black man playing lead guitar in a rock band or singing lead as a "Rock & Roller" like Elvis seemed bizarre. The standard narrative became that white rock musicians were guided by an individual creative vision, whereas black musicians were considered authentic only when they stayed true to black traditions. Serious rock became white because only white musicians could be original without accusations of racial betrayal.

By the 1980s, rock music produced and performed by African Americans was no longer considered "authentically black"—not to audiences and in particular within the music industry. The prevailing sentiment was that neither black audiences, white audiences nor black musicians—had any interest in black rock.

So when and, more importantly, *why* did rock & roll become "white" music when its roots are so steeped in black culture? And how did it affect Little Richard, the African American progenitor of the genre who was still performing it?

There is a short story by Alice Walker called *Nineteen Fifty-Five* where a man named Traynor, who is the "King of Rock & Roll", tells the protagonist, Gracie Mae Still, an older black songwriter from whom he has bought songs cheaply over the years which she had recorded. Traynor made the songs into hits by re-recording them as 'white-bread' covers. Says Traynor to Gracie:

"They want what you got but they don't want you. They want what I got only it ain't mine. That's what makes 'em so hungry for me when I sing. They getting the flavor of something but they ain't getting the thing itself. They like a pack of hound dogs trying to gobble up a scent."[12]

Yes, it is a thinly veiled rendering of Elvis Presley and Willie Mae "Big Mama" Thornton, the black woman who wrote (and sang) 'Hound Dog.' But more importantly, it completely defines the dilemma all too many songwriters and singers of color experienced in those days as their works were bought on the cheap, or co-opted and re-packaged for white audiences, but were not given their proper credit or financial due for having created the music. It illustrates the reality of a business that was compelled to, as writer Charles Shaar Murray wrote, "separate black music (which, by and large, white Americans love) from black people (who, by and large, white Americans don't)."[13]

Yes, Little Richard was angered by what the music power structure did to him in his day, but he didn't simmer in silence—not then. Not now. He demanded fairer treatment but in the end he believed that racism robbed him of his musical legacy. During a 1999 interview with the Washington Post, Richard still touted himself as "The Architect of Rock & Roll." He said:

> I put blues and boogie-woogie together and made rock & roll. I'm the architect of rock & roll; I created it. ...It's just rhythm and blues up-tempo. It's just that old blues beat speeded up with more bottom on it. It's black music, but they won't admit it. They won't give us credit. If it's a white guy, they say he's the King of Rock & Roll, but if it's a black guy, they add 'self-proclaimed'; they say he's the 'self-proclaimed King of Rock & Roll.' Well, if it's pork, say it comes from the pig. If it's beef, say it comes from the cow. If it's rock 'n' roll, say it comes from black people.[14]

Preach, brother. Sitting before Paul McCartney on-stage at the 1988 Rock & Roll Hall of Fame induction ceremony of The Beatles, Richard said it almost made him cry not to be acknowledged by Paul who had often blatantly mimicked him on so many Beatles records. Later Paul was exonerated by George Harrison who pointed to Little Richard and said: *"Thank you all very much, especially the rock 'n' rollers, an' Little Richard there, if it wasn't for* [gesturing to Richard], *it was all his fault, really."*[15]

Two decades earlier, Little Richard stood alone amongst the most influential rock & roll performers whose audiences were primarily young white kids. His influence on musicians of his time was unparalleled, and these artists were some of the giants in the industry.

But what about Little Richard himself? Just *who* was this mastermind who created Rock & Roll? What made him tick? What lay beneath the make-up, capes, costumes and outrageousness?

In my quest to delve inside the psyche and genesis of his music, persona, and southern Baptist roots, I discovered a reality. Behind Little Richard's flamboyance and incredible onstage presence—which has been lovingly "borrowed" by so many—there was an epic ongoing personal battle. One he struggled with all throughout his career—his complicated relationship with his sexual orientation, and its effect on his Christian faith.

Half a dozen times in his life, Richard left secular music to lift his voice "for the Lord" in an effort to suppress his homosexuality.

In an interview on the Christian-oriented Three Angels Broadcasting Network in 2017, Little Richard reiterated his belief that homosexuality was *"unnatural"* while reaffirming his strong Christian faith that had followed him for most of his life. *"God made men, men—and women, women... You've got to live the way God wants you to live... He can save you."*[16]

But a year later, he was back on stage strutting his stuff, shakin' his ass singing *Tutti Frutti,* a song originating as a testament to homosexuality.

A writer who once sat face-to-face with Little Richard, found his thoughts turning to the things Richard's eyes have seen in his life—images he was told were: church congregations observing Richard preaching in a way that led one worshipper to describe Richard as "the most Christ-like figure I have ever met"; a friend of Richard's leading a naked man around a dressing room by a penis *"so long that it looked like a towrope"*; a low-flying Soviet satellite which persuaded the singer Armageddon was imminent so he must quit performing; and countless orgies distinguished by degrees of athleticism, stamina and ingenuity so remarkable that, if Richard's own memory is to be trusted, they might have shocked the Marquis de Sade.[17]

"I remember one night," said Richard to his first biographer, Charles White *"we had this wonderful orgy going. One of the best I have ever been to. And in the middle of it...* somebody knocked on my door. I said: 'Just a moment! This is an orgy!'"[18]

Little Richard has long publicly fought a battle between his faith and sexuality, but something about this man who, as of this writing, has not walked in years due to a bad hip made me feel like this battle may finally be over. These days there is no eyeliner, makeup, or wigs. The high-energy of the performer is absent.

But neither God, nor Little Richard won. The violence he went through as a child, and the rigid laws and attitudes surrounding sexuality and gender we socialize people into accepting, is the victor. And this is far too often our black male musical icons' narrative.

Most black people are born into an Abrahamic religion. But very often artistic inquisitiveness contradicts the laws of that religion. But artistic expression *must* be articulated. That articulation, in this case, was Rock & Roll expressed through the art of a queer black man—an aesthetic that shifted how we see our stars, gay or straight. It's David Bowie in sequins and full makeup. It's Michael Jackson with sequined socks, gloves and fedora. It's Freddie Mercury in capes and crowns, Elton John in huge sunglasses and platform shoes, Lady Gaga in meat dresses—and Prince in, well, anything.

These stars and their expressions freed young white people, generation after generation, but imprisoned Little Richard inside of his own black guilt because he had a deep rooted belief that his gayness, thus his music, was against God who gave him his talent in the first place.

It is sad to think that the people who created the Grunge movement in the 70s, rap in the 80s, hip hop in the 90s, or the Afropunk music fests in the 2000s have not all been able to receive the same type of societal freedom for their differentness.

In the case of Little Richard, what we have now is a man who designed a magnificent art form that made us happy. It made me—as a young girl who would go on to have her *own* creative expression—sing and dance up and down the hall as a kid.

But then Richard restrained himself with religion when he should have enhanced and exalted himself with it. God gave him a larger than life gift—one very few of us would have dismissed or written off to the "devil."

For a man of God, now older, wiser, and a recluse, Little Richard's experiences, decisions and memories—many gleaned from his extraordinary career and various interviews—reveal a journey fraught with indecision, confusion and epic, candid, confrontations between his outer affectations—and his inner demons.

That legendary career incorporates a remarkable life spent in the parallel universes of the sacred, the secular, and the sexual...

...And it is a story that *must* be told.

Tina Andrews
New York City, 2020

Prologue

The "Event"

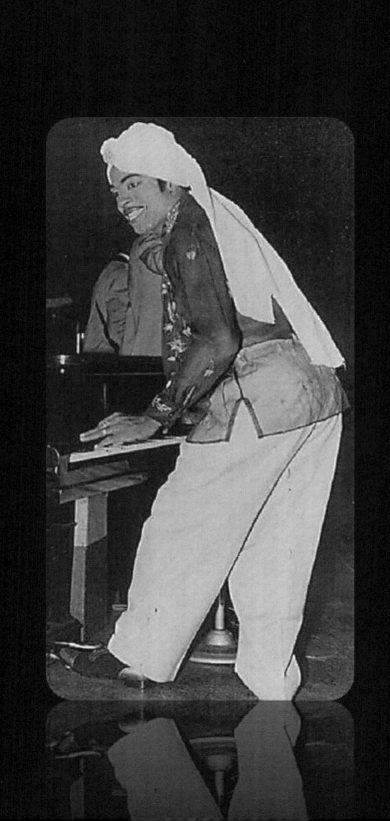

It was October 9, 1985. The tour in Britain had been grueling. Little Richard had just recorded his first all-new album in eight years, *Lifetime Friends,* that seemed to merge the two disparate forces in his life—flagrant rock & roll exhibitionism, and sacred Christian morality—both of which resulted from his dueling roles as a gay showbusiness performer and an evangelist gospel singer/ preacher.

After completing work on the album in London, things were not helped by an eleven hour flight back to Los Angeles on Oct. 8, 1985 followed by 12 hours filming on the set of NBC's hit television drama *Miami Vice* where he had just wrapped playing the character of "Reverend Marvelle Quinn," a minister preaching the gospel against drug abuse beachside in Miami. The episode, titled *"Where the Buses Don't Run"* would be broadcast in the series' second season.

Richard was exhausted. He was in the middle of a stunning Hollywood comeback and so many people were cheering on his success. In addition to recording the album, he had made a music video; recently filmed the movie *Down and Out in Beverly Hills* where he sang his hit *Great Gosh A'Mighty* and made guest appearances on *The Tonight Show* starring Johnny Carson and *The Hollywood Squares*. On top of this he had been chosen by the Rock & Roll Hall of Fame as one of their first ever inductees; and he was planning another world tour.

All Richard wanted now...was some sleep.

Driving back from the set sometime after midnight on Santa Monica Boulevard's route 66 on his way to the hotel where he was living, Richard fell asleep at the wheel of his Nissan 300ZX traveling 60 miles per hour. He lost control of the car and, in one spectacular display of unexpected bad luck, smashed into a telephone pole on Curson Avenue.

The impact nearly killed him. Firefighters and paramedics came and it took over an hour for them to cut the living legend from the wreckage with the Jaws of Life. Richard, 52 years old at the time, was unconscious—pinned between the steering wheel and front seat.

He was so seriously injured he should've died given the severity of the crash. His right leg had to be reconstructed as it was fractured in eight places, and the singer also suffered a punctured bladder, broken ribs, and head and facial injuries.

The accident prevented him from being able to attend the inaugural Rock & Roll Hall of Fame ceremony on January 23, 1986 where he was among the first group of ten to ever be inducted in the new organization and appear on its first televised show. When he was finally able, Little Richard had to send a videotaped message to his fans in acceptance of his induction since, sadly, it would take the singer another six months to recover.

But for Richard, it was enough time to take stock of his existence—to contemplate his career and the duality of his life's purpose. To reflect on his journey from Macon, Georgia as a teenaged boy who sang gospel in church while struggling with feelings of same-sex attraction, who went on to become one of the biggest stars in the world forever known as:

"The Architect of Rock & Roll."

As he wandered in and out of consciousness—his soul was in an untethered, spectral state of "Am I alive, or should I just die" purgatory. He had the time to remember and deconstruct that young boy; that black kid growing up in segregated Georgia who was so eager to succeed through an insurmountable quantity of obstacles: Emotional, regretful, external, internal...

...and spiritual.

Side "A"

Sex, Drugs, Rock 'n' Roll

"My inspiration for singing was Mahalia Jackson. She sang with so much feeling. She was so sincere; she inspired me quite a bit. When you hear my show in person, if you listen closely, you can hear her in me. My phrasing is different, because I was singing rock & roll, but I used how she put feeling in a song, how she would lose herself in a song."

—Little Richard

One

Macon, Georgia

'**G**od, sin, and music. That's what I was born into," said Little Richard who began singing in his local church choir while still a youngster because musical tastes in his household were limited. Richard recalled he "came from a family where my people didn't like rhythm & blues. It was either Bing Crosby's *Pennies From Heaven,* or Ella Fitzgerald. That's all I heard."[19]

But Little Richard was also born into a world defined by a larger separatism. A world divided by blackness and whiteness. The "twoness," as W. E. B. DuBois wrote in *The Souls of Black Folk,* in which it was impossible to avoid "this sense of always looking at one's self through the eyes of others, of measuring one's soul by the tape of a predominantly white society that looks on in amused contempt and pity."[20]

And yet, it was also a world, as Du Bois determined, which was so rich, vibrant and colorful, that giving in to its own devices, created a culture that defined a sector of the American artistic mainstream. This sector encompassed a community of artists in which imagination and self-invention could triumph over pedigree, and in which, as James Baldwin wrote in *The Fire Next Time*, there existed:

> "...*a zest and a joy and a capacity for facing and surviving disaster... Perhaps we were, all of us, pimps, whores, racketeers, church members, and children— bound together by the nature of our oppression, the specific and peculiar complex of risks we had to run.*"[21]

This "*complex of risks*" coupled with that "*imagination*" and "*self-invention*" were born into Richard Wayne Penniman as given to him by the *Creator of all things.*

Young "Lil" Richard Penniman

Raised in Macon, Georgia, the third of the twelve children born to Leva Mae and Charles "Bud" Penniman, Richard arrived on the scene on December 5, 1932. His father, a church deacon, was a stern disciplinarian who also owned a nightclub called the Tip-In Inn and sold moonshine as a bootlegger on the side when prohibition ruled.

From an early age he showed interest in music, singing and playing the piano in his local church, absorbing the blues and gospel music of his deep Southern heritage.

Though Richard grew up dirt poor, he also grew up in a variety of Christian denominations, all of them leaning toward the conservative end of the spectrum. This included Baptist, Pentecostal, Holiness, African Methodist Episcopal (AME) and Seventh Day Adventist churches. In these religious venues, he would certainly have seen many models for his charismatic, public future.

"Lil" Richard, as he was known as a child, and his family were in church every Sunday. It was de rigueur. No ifs, ands, or buts about it. Saturday night Leva Mae cooked dinner. Then the family would all get up around 6:30 on Sunday morning because everyone had to take their bath, and there were a lot of them and only one bathroom. They would be dressed and at church for nine o'clock Sunday school, and afterward, the eleven o'clock regular service with prayer and singing. Richard liked the singing best. When he led the choir with *Yes, Jesus Loves Me*, the church ladies waved their cardboard hand fans in the air, and people nodded with pure enjoyment, and congratulated Richard's parent's afterward. It Was the only occasion when he felt he could please his father, Bud. For someone so young he had a remarkable voice which enthralled the congregation. Because of his youthful leanings toward earthly temptations, secular music was discouraged in his house. In fact, his family had strict rules against playing R&B music, which they considered "devil music." In an era before downloads, MTV, VH1, Pandora, Spotify, YouTube, or customized playlists on iPhones, one heard music on vinyl albums, 45 records on a record player, a jukebox, or the radio. Nothing was digital. It was all analogue.

> *We didn't have nothing to play records on, 'cause we were real poor," Richard remembered. "My mother had 12 children, so we didn't have nothing. We had an old radio we would play late at night. We would listen to WLAC out of Tennessee. Back in that time boogie-woogie was very popular. I would say that boogie-woogie and rhythm & blues mixed is rock & roll. Also, back in that time black people were singing a lot of country music."*[22]

Young Richard would have to wait until external influences eventually found him from outside musical sources that would excite him. A ninth-grade dropout with dreams of becoming as popular as the singing evangelist Brother Joe May, known as "the Thunderbolt of the Midwest," Richard loved and was inspired by the black gospel greats of the '30s and '40s. There was fellow Georgian, Ray Charles and he especially loved Mahalia Jackson and borrowed from her style as often as possible. He would say:

My inspiration for singing was Mahalia Jackson. She sang with so much feeling. She was so sincere; she inspired me quite a bit. When you hear my show in person, if you listen closely, you can hear her in me. My phrasing is different, because I was singing rock & roll, but I used how she put a feeling in a song, how she would lose herself in a song.[23]

One of the things he enjoyed doing was hanging out at the Macon City Auditorium where he saw Cab Calloway and other celebrities perform. In addition to Mahalia Jackson there were several female singers who caught his attention as well such as Sister Rosetta Tharpe and Marion Williams of the Clara Ward Singers. When he was age 13, Williams invited him to the stage to sing with her in a local appearance, and from then on, he wanted to pursue music as a livelihood.

But Richard was also growing up as a young black man during one of the most turbulent, racist, segregated eras in American history save for slavery. Dwight and Mamie Eisenhower were in the White House, the Ku Klux Klan ran the south and were rarely provoked, and white southerners had a deep seated hatred for blacks. Richard dealt with "White Only" or "Colored Only" water fountains and restaurants, and more than once saw a bereft family remove the body of a loved one from a tree after a lynching, or witnessed white policemen beat and then push black men into squad cars and haul them off to jail for no apparent reason except being on the street.

Such behavior instills feelings of perpetual fear and low self-esteem when one cannot give agency to one's own God-given freedom to be. You always keep one eye behind you for you never know when it will be your turn to be the recipient of racist acts beyond your control.

The geography of the black section of Macon in 1947 was primarily along the railroad tracks. Shanty houses and lean-to's, mostly built on concrete blocks with wobbly, occasionally rotting wood stairs, would shake as the train roared by twice a day. There were no streetlights or paved thoroughfares. They were all dirt roads which were muddy for days after a bad rain.

In the deep south back then, most blacks were off the streets by 9pm. There was no such thing as hotels, restaurants or bars that accepted "Negroes." If you were black and visiting, you had to have a relative or friend to stay with or sleep in a "Negro boardinghouse" and make sure you were there by the unwritten code of conduct for the black curfew. This was how Little Richard grew up.

However, Richard described the music that *he* would hear amidst the squalor around him—sounds that inspired his music—women washing clothes, laughter and idle gossip on corners, raking leaves. People sang as they went about their lives and Richard described it fondly:

> There wasn't any rock & roll at that time... So we sang gospel. Everybody around us was singing gospel—the women hanging out the wash, the old men on the porches at night, everybody.[24]

In 1986 on the Southbank Show in the UK, Richard elaborated:

> When I was a little boy, you would hear black people singing all over the neighborhood, singing spirituals, you know, like *'nobody knows the trouble. I see'* or *'Sometimes I feel like a motherless child.'* And you would hear a black person way over here singing the song. Then you hear another black person way over here singing the song. And they all sing it. In unison. You know, just everybody harmonize it. And then late at night, I would run down the street singing a song called 'Hitch It To Wagon and Pull the Line.' I would do that late at night at twelve o'clock. Nobody wanted to kill me in the neighborhood."

Richard expounded his story for Rolling Stone Magazine in 1970:

"Then there used to be a man comin' around singin', beatin' a washboard... an' singin':

> *Bam-a-lam-bam*
> *You shall be free*
> *In the mornin'*
> *You shall be free*

I'd follow him around, goin', *'Bam-a-lam-bam/You shall be free,'* Then the vegetable man would come by. He would draw the people out and he would sing:

Blackeyed peas
And a barrel of beans
Grocer man comin'
with a cart of greens, Honey.

And people would all come to the door, and the man
would be ridin' down the street with a horse, a wagon,
and singin' and everybody would come to the door,
and he'd just keep singin,'

Blackeyed peas
And a barrel of beans
Grocer man comin'
with cart of greens, Honey.

It was really somethin'. Everybody be singin' and we
never practiced: it was a big choir like fifty voices all
over the neighborhood, and that's what I came from.[25]

From a young age Richard learned that both blacks
and whites enjoyed hearing a good voice and he realized
that blacks who had musical ability sometimes got a
"Hail Mary" pass from white oppression. White people
loved black music whether secretly or outright. It was an
equalizer and common language within humanity.

But given Richard's talent, he wrestled with many
other internal conflicts he wanted to overcome. He had
been born with a deformity. His right leg was 3 inches
shorter than his left giving him a noticeable limp. It made
him look like he was sashaying when he walked. Other

kids would bully and chase him into the woods calling him "faggot," "punk," "freak," and "sissy boy."

"Kids called me every homophobic slur. But I guess I always knew I was different. I just didn't know what it meant back then."

In hopes of curing Richard's birth defect, his mother, Leva Mae sent him to New Hope Baptist Church every Sunday. There he discovered a talent for singing. His leg never lengthened, but his lungs got lots of exercise. At church Richard learned he had a hell of a voice.[26]

Hell—being the operative word.

Richard had an infectious, hyperactive personality that was contagious and made him popular. But it also got him into trouble and his leanings toward homosexuality didn't helps—especially with his father.

Bud Penniman was embarrassed by his son's mincing affectations thus Richard had a troubled relationship with his father. Bud would regularly whip and verbally abuse the boy—even though Richard later credited his father's strict discipline with playing a large role in his success.

In the early days, as a teenager, Richard would watch his mother put on her make-up in the bureau mirror and he would want to put make-up on too. When his mother wasn't at home, he would sneak in her room and put on her high heels and walked around in them. Then he'd go into her drawer and get out her lipstick and pancake make-up and put it all over his face.

He liked how he looked.

When Richard became an older teenager, he came under the spell of two men who would have a great impact on his onstage presence, appearance and performance style—Billy Wright, a local blues singer from New Orleans, and Esquerita, a singer, songwriter and pianist from Greenville, South Carolina.

When Richard met Billy Wright in 1952 he was immediately taken with Wright's appearance. Wright wore pomade in his hair that was piled high on his

head into a pompadour with "conk," and he donned himself in flashy clothes. But it was Wright's stage make-up of eyeliner and face powder that really caught Richard's attention.

Wright had worked as a dancer and female impersonator, but ultimately developed as a singer when he began performing at Atlanta's 81 Theater. He

Billy Wright, circa 1950 with gold teeth and pompadour

worked the tent shows in drag, a great southern, show biz tradition in itself and an important influence on rock 'n' roll—hence the term "tent show queen."

He sang the repertoire of that tradition—which was a true underground movement of its time—and sang many of the tunes Little Richard heard, rewrote, and later cleaned up with which he went to the bank, e.g., *Tutti*

Frutti (whose original lyrics were: *"Tutti Frutti/Good bootie/if it don't fit/don't force it/just grease it/make it easy"*); *Busy Bootin'* aka *Keep A Knockin'*; and *Don't You Want A Man Like Me*, etc.

In the early 1950s when most queer men were in the closet with the door securely locked, only coming out at gay bars and clubs in metropolitan cities, Billy Wright was an open and unapologetic homosexual. It was something the young Richard who was just coming to grips with his own gayness wished he could embrace. Wright helped Richard establish a stage look, advising him to use pancake makeup and wear his hair in a big pompadour style similar to his own.[27] Richard, the enamored, dutiful student, borrowed everything from Wright—especially his extensive make-up style which almost became a requirement for playing in white clubs where being a Black man in make-up and weird hair rendered them sexually harmless. It was also, for Richard, a great excuse for his cross-dressing leanings.

Wright would later describe Penniman as "the most fantastic entertainer he had ever seen"; and of Wright, Little Richard repeated the same thing.[28] Listening to Wright's recordings it's not hard to hear just how much Richard's singing style was based on Wright's. Then, if you throw in Clara Ward's "wooo's" and Esquerita's piano pounding rhythm, you have Little Richard's entire oeuvre.

Esquerita, circa 1952

As for Esquerita, Richard's second inspiration, the story goes that while Billy was on the road, Richard began to hang out in the gay section of Macon where he soon developed a taste for voyeurism. He would go to the Greyhound Bus station where, by Richard's own admission, he lingered longer than most in the men's room so he could look at men's penises as they urinated. This is where he met Esquerita, a local musician, and another openly gay black man with a pompadour hairdo.

Esquerita—whose real name was Steve Quincy Reeder Jr.—adopted his stage name for its scatological sound *"SQReeder"*. He was a piano celebrity who had recorded early rock and roll music for a new Capitol Records. He employed a unique piano playing style and became an earnest ally who proved crucial for Richard's soon-to-be distinctive keyboard skills—skills which became integral in his dazzling stage personality. Esquerita, taught Richard an array of visually impressive piano techniques, most of which involved rapidly repeating, high-volume stock passages and chords in the upper treble region of the piano.

With this newly acquired skill, Richard would attract greater attention in his early struggles to get started and achieve some fame along the way for breaking more than his share of pianos strings, partnered with his "genuinely outrageous personality."[29]

Esquerita suggested that Richard get a wig for the pompadour look he wanted while his own hair was growing out in order to get a "conk"—the chemical lye process that black men used to straighten their hair texture so it could be worn in an upright pompadour. Esquerita was notoriously promiscuous and would become, in the early 1960s, a popular recording artist in his own right.

Sadly, when he died of AIDS in the mid-1980s he was washing windscreens for tips at a Brooklyn intersection.[30]

Sister Rosetta Tharpe

Employing Esquerita's advice, Richard went into a downtown Macon wig shop and tried on one or two wigs. But he didn't buy one until after, it so happened, he was walking past The Macon City Auditorium and saw a crew unloading cars and setting up equipment. He asked who was performing. When told it was Sister Rosetta Tharpe, Richard knew he had to meet her. Sister Rosetta was considered "The Godmother of Soul" and Richard's favorite.

When he saw Sister Rosetta step out of her Cadillac headed to the Stage Door entrance, he ran up in front of her and started singing one of her songs, *"Two Little Fish and Five Loaves of Bread."* Sister Rosetta grinned. "Boy, where you learn to sing like that? You wanna come up on stage tonight an' sing a song with me?" Richard was in shock but nodded.

Richard's father
Charles "Bud" Penniman

Later, during the show, Sister Rosetta invited Little Richard up to sing and the two were hilarious, but more importantly, fabulous as they sang *"I want a Tall Skinny Papa."* Everybody applauded and cheered. *"It was the best thing that had ever happened to me,"* said Richard. *"Sister Rosetta gave me $30-$40 dollars, and I'd never had so much money in my life before."*[31]

Richard bought that wig—perhaps because he had just received money from Sister Rosetta. But we do not know when he fully embraced wearing wigs and pancake make-up. What we do know is that his father hated Richard's effeminate behavior and burgeoning homosexuality.

And yet, Bud Penniman had his own nefarious activities going on that were illegal and may have affected his son.

[D]addy used to sell moonshine liquor, and the police were always trying to catch him with the stuff in the house. I remember one night at about one o'clock in the morning, I had been to the store, singing at the top of my voice going down those muddy roads, and I had just got home when the police came. Daddy was inside with some people. He was selling whisky when the policemen knocked at our door, and I went to see who was there. Daddy had made a triple screen so that you could see out but nobody could see in. The police just slammed the door back. They knocked a big knot in my head. And they searched the place. Somehow Daddy had got the people out. They got away. The police went through the bedrooms anyway and pulled the covers off the kids to see if there was any whisky in the bed with them! Daddy used to hide the jugs of bootleg whisky at Miz Stafford's next door. She had a big garden with collard greens in it. He used to pay her and bury the jugs there in the garden, putting the greens back over them, and watering them down so you'd never know nothin' was buried under there. And the neighbors would never tell on him, because he was very generous and kind to the kids. I guess that's why he never got caught."[32]

Richard at age 14 was always in trouble at school. He had a lack of interest in his studies, and he was recalcitrant at home and mischievous. He did things that were simply bizarre. For instance, once he put his bowel movements in a shoebox and wrapped it up like a present then gave it to an old lady who lived next to grocery store in Macon on her birthday. Imagine how she felt when she opened it.

Indeed Richard Penniman was at the first crossroad of his life. He admitted to hanging around the traveling shows that came to town and he'd sing with them. He liked the gay crowd in Macon and was growing more and more comfortable with them—even to the point of telling his mother about it.

> I used to tell my mother about the gay scene and she used to tell me to hush. I'd tell her about the words they would use and how they'd call everybody "Miss Thing." Anybody meeting you—meeting another guy—would say "child." "How you doin', child." And you'd go, "How you doin', honey ... "What happened last night, Miss Thing?" I'd call Billy Wright's and say, "How's Billy doin', Miss Thing?" and he'd say, "She's fine ... Oh honey, you should see her now.[33]

Leva Mae Penniman

Some part of Leva Mae had to know her son was gay (as most mothers of same-sex loving children generally do), and she may have turned a blind eye toward it. But she showed Richard nothing but affection. Richard adored her and loved that she pushed him toward a musical career, albeit one in the church.

However, Richard's father was always critical of his son for the way he walked and talked, and for the people Richard was associating with. Bud Penniman was cruel to Richard. He berated and degraded the teenager for acting feminine. "He would get real mad at me, and then hit me. But I couldn't help it. That was the way I was."[34]

Sometimes Richard wore his mother's curtains and proclaimed himself "the Magnificent One." These charmingly glamorous antics infuriated Bud, who as a church deacon was a firm believer in gender norms. He not only insulted his son but rabidly attacked him.

The night he saw Richard in make-up and a wig, Bud had had enough. He told Richard "My father had seven sons and I wanted seven sons. But you've spoiled it. You're only half a son!"[35] Then he wiped off Richard's face, stripped off the teenager's clothes, and savagely beat him naked and tied to a chair.

These beatings went on for most of Richard's young life. Little Richard gave Jet Magazine an interview in 2003 about those beatings:

> ...I could feel the licks. My dad would tie me to the bed and beat me with switches. He would tie my hands to the top of the bed and my feet too, and beat me butt naked. My back would be split open, blood coming out. The skin was torn loose. But I endured. [36]

Most likely it was his mother who stopped the uncon-
scionable assaults. But for Bud, Richard was dead to him.
Ultimately, when viciously pulverizing his son didn't
work that night, Bud banished Richard from the house
altogether. There was no room in his home, his community, his heart—and especially his church—for Richard's
developing queer lifestyle.

Richard was 15.

Little Richard and Chuck Berry, 1971

Two

Death and Dreams Deferred

There was not much a teenager could do out in the world to ensure his own survival. Rejected by his father and harassed by hostile bigots, he was fortunate to ultimately find acceptance with a white couple named Ann and Johnny Johnson who owned the Tick Tock Club in Macon. They happily took him in. Both were Seventh Day Adventists.

In this entirely new sphere of influence, he was to learn all he could have ever wanted from the secular musical entertainment life. In various interviews, Little Richard confirmed that he was sexually active with both women and men beginning in his early teens; he would evolve into participation in sexual orgies and voyeurism later.[37] But thanks to the Johnsons he was given a home. In fact, a song Richard later wrote, *Miss Ann,* was written about her.

At the time, in Richard's young life, there was a very good-looking gay man named Bobby who caught

Richard's eye. They met in Clarksville, Tennessee, at a club called the Queens City Rainbow. He was a female impersonator, and he looked just like a woman.

> There was a soldier base not far from there called Fort Campbell, Kentucky. I used to go and play and Bobby would put on these dresses and the hair and go on stage. The soldiers would scream and go mad. You see at that time he had a shape. Bobby was very bold. He would walk by the dressing rooms leading his boyfriend by the penis, which was just like a rope. Bobby liked to be at Fort Campbell and accost the soldiers, to sell his body to them. Bobby would come back sometimes, with the heels broken off his shoes 'cos those guys would have run him down the street when they found out they'd been with a man. They'd be playing with you and they'd reach down and they'd be just smilin'—and then all of a sudden... But some guys were pleased, you know?[38]

There was also man who profoundly affected Richard. His name was Doctor Nobilio, and he was the Macon town prophet who wore a turban and a red-and-yellow cape and carried a black stick. Richard began performing with him in 1949 and was inspired to wear capes and turbans himself. Said Richard,

> I'd sing to attract the people and then he'd prophesy. People would come to see 'the thing' he carried about with him. He called it the Devil's Child. It was the dried-up body of a baby with claw feet like a bird

and horns on its head... Doctor Nobilio was a spirit-
ualist... He told me, 'Boy, you're gonna be famous,
but you're gonna have to go where the grass is
greener!'[39]

After Richard was with the Johnson's for a while, he
left to join the Dr. Hudson's Medicine Show. Doc Hudson
was from Macon and sold snake oil. His talent was for
going into towns, gathering all the black people, and telling them that the snake oil was the cure for everything.
They believed him and bought tons of snake-oil—hence
the term "Snake-oil salesman."

...He was lying," Richard laughed to biographer Charles
White. "Snake oil! I was helping him lie. Doc Hudson,
he'd go in cryin', 'Everybody come here. I got snake oil.
If you got rheumatism, arthritis, if you got leg trouble,
if you got toe trouble—this bottle's good for everything."
Two dollars a bottle. He had a stage out in the open, and
a feller by the name of James would play piano. In the
show, I would sing, *'Cal'donia, Cal'donia, what makes
your big head so hard.'* It was by Louis Jordan an' it was
the only song I knew that wasn't a church song.[40]

Richard spent much of his remaining teenaged years
traveling across the state in various traveling medicine
and minstrel show troupes including those of Sugar Foot
Sam as well as Doc Hudson. He helped Doc Hudson sell
snake oil for a long time before later joining various other
traveling bands, sometimes performing in drag as "Princess Lavonne." He performed with bands like Percy

Welch, and one night in Fitzgerald, Georgia, Richard vis-
ited a local jook joint to catch a rhythm and blues act

named "B. Brown
and His Orchestra."
Before they were to
begin, the group's
vocalist had fallen
sick and Richard
was encouraged to
sit in. His powerful,
wailing voice seized
everyone's attention,

The 'Dolls" at the Drag shows in and around Atlanta. Circa 1950

including Brown, who after the show asked Richard to
join his band. The 15 year old singer accepted and soon
became the group's featured act, taking the stage name
"Little" Richard given him by Brown because as he was
only five foot-ten including the pompadour hairdo, and
because of his youth. The young entertainer dazzled audiences throughout the southern chitlin' circuit.

The work he did during that time even included dancing as he was hired for one tour to attract customers to
the stage for Sugarfoot Sam's Minstrel Show. Other trav-
els included a stint of employment with vaudeville star
Spencer "Smoke" Anthony.

In a short time, Richard came back to Macon as a wise
veteran of audience dynamics and a smooth manipulator
on the stage. Richard's career as a traveling musician—
and his life as a sexually adventurous, gender-bending
wild man had begun. He sexually experimented with

men in the gay underworld in Macon, guys named Madame Oop and Sis Henry and Bro Boy, as well as with older women. In those first quasi-professional years, Richard spent time with various bands and ensembles, such as the Tempo Toppers, the Upsetters, and Voices That Care. The Upsetters would eventually become his ongoing backup band.

The year 1951 that would mark the beginning for the career of "Little Richard." He won a talent contest held on Atlanta radio backed by a band led by Billy Wright, who recommended Little Richard to RCA Victor. Richard landed a short-term contract there with additional help from Zenas Sears, a white disc jockey who loved a wide range of music and helped many notable African-American performers to their next career steps.

RCA, Richard's first label, got Richard into the studio at Radio WGST where all-in he cut a total of eight tracks: *I Brought It All On Myself, Thinkin' 'Bout My Mother, Please Have Mercy On Me,* and *Ain't Nothin' Happening*—the only one that gave the world a glimpse of the excitement to come.

Later, he would also record songs such as *Taxi Blues, Every Hour,* and *Get Rich Quick* which were essentially impersonations of Billy Wright. But none of these earlier recordings made a profound impression on the record-buying public, and while he was in Houston, his contract with RCA Victor expired. So Richard, feeling a bit dejected, returned home to Macon—to the Johnsons—and continued his one-night stands with the Upsetters, his back-up band, or the Percy Welch Orchestra. Yet Little Richard would not realize his true professional identity for a while.

For a long time, Little Richard had been praying for the ability to forgive his father, and for his father to forgive him. He prayed that Bud would accept both him and his music because little by little, Richard was coming into his own as a performer.

Then he received a surprise. Bud Penniman showed up at one of Richard's performances in Macon. When they met backstage, Bud smiled and told his son he was proud of him, and that he had one of his records in the jukebox at the his club Tip-In Inn. He said he played it all the time. Bud even offered to buy Richard a better car the following Monday since the Chrysler Richard was driving was in such poor shape. Said Richard:

> My daddy had never been behind me in my career un-
> til then, and he was just starting to come behind me.
> He was going to buy me a car ...to help me in my trav-
> eling. But he never gave me that car...[41]

...Because tragedy struck. On a rainy Tuesday night, February 12, 1952, Bud Penniman was shot outside the Tip In Inn. He knew the man who shot him. His name was Frank Tanner and he came from a family with a bad reputation in Macon. Frank was shooting firecrackers into the coal stove that heated the room. Bud had asked Frank to stop, but he didn't. So Bud Penniman told Frank to get out of the bar. Tanner and his friends started a rukus outside the club and Bud got his pistol and went out. Frank Tanner shot him. Bud Penniman was dead before they could get him to the hospital.

Richard had been away at the time, but his sister Peggy was in the club at the time and witnessed it all. By the time Richard heard the news and ran home, all he saw was his father's bloody raincoat lying on the porch.

In 1987, Richard told writer/director John Waters:

> A raincoat with all this blood on it. It was just... something. I walked in the door, seein' my mother. I looked at this beautiful woman and she said: 'Bru?' My mother called me Bru and I called her Mu. She said: 'Bru?' and I said: 'What is it, Mu?' She said: 'You don't have no more dad,' and I just cried. 'Oh, no! Lord!' Everything inside me just broke. 'Cause my mother, that's my heart. When my mother cried, boy, that shakes my mind! I can do some drastic things behind Mu! I ain't scared of lions, tigers, snakes, puppy-dog tail, or chickens! It [segregation] was so hard then. But you still had a peace, a serenity: that joy, that hope, that determination, that perseverance that some day, somehow, I *will* make it![42]

Richard has told many reporters over the years that he believed someone had his father killed.

They didn't keep Frank in jail, and we were too poor. We couldn't get no lawyer and fight it. We believe that the police didn't like him because ... that's all I can say. I just believe that somebody had him killed, that's all... My mother took it very hard because she was pregnant at the time. I remember going back to Macon in 1962 or 1963, and Frank Tanner coming to us and asking us to forgive him, and we did.[43]

The Tip In Inn was a small club that looked like a café. It was one room and they sold food, beer and wine. There was a jukebox and the young people would go and dance and have fun. The night of the shooting, Peggie Penniman, Richard's sister, happened to be there and was talking to her father, Bud Richard's record was on the jukebox and kids were dancing to it. According to Peggy, Bud played it all the time and was very proud of it.

Some say eighteen-year-old Frank Tanner was known to Richard's future adopted son. Others say Richard and Frank were friends and that the incident probably came about because of a drug or gambling transaction. Nonetheless, Frank Tanner was out of jail in a week, and Richard's family thought the entire incident was suspect. The police were not interested in the murder of a black man, and Richard's mother, a soft-spoken, God-fearing, very pregnant Leva Mae Penniman, did not have the money to pursue a case.

So whether the police were in cahoots with Frank because Bud Penniman sold moonshine illegally, or it was a drug transaction gone sour, the family never found out what really happened—and in one shocking act, Richard lost the man who gave him life, but made that life a nightmare. And the scars his father left, remained.

Now needing money to support his large family, 19-year-old Richard Penniman moved back into the family home. For Little Richard, any notion of going on more extensive tours, trifling around, cross-dressing and showboating with traveling minstrels had to end. No more glitchy little jukebox records that no one bought bringing no future with it. Nor could he think about relocating far from Macon. That all ended when Charles "Bud" Penniman was shot to death outside of his bar.

There were now 12 in the house to feed. With his older brother Charles off fighting in Korea, Richard assumed the role of breadwinner. He would have to have a regular income, and if that meant scrubbing dishes (or whatever it took) so be it—because his family needed him.

Thus, Little Richard got a job washing dishes at the Greyhound bus station in Macon to make the families ends meet.

During this pressurized, unhappy time, Richard would sometimes perform at Ann and Johnnie's Tick Tock Club. But mostly he washed dishes in the bus terminal kitchen during the day—singing to himself to pass the time.

In the months after his father's death, Richard's life and dreams seemed to move in slow motion. And yet, the vision he had for a career for himself in music was not dead.

As he scrubbed dishes at the Greyhound depot, Richard observed the humanity around him.

There is no telling how all of it manifested in his music or his psyche, but his new life experience included ingesting everything from the shady characters of the Jim Crow South who passed through his orbit; bigots who cursed him, the homeless, segregationists, evangelists, celibates, soldiers and policemen. A whole cast of colorful characters cruised through that bus station after dark when the whole town was dead.

Writer Robert Chalmers said the only man ever to claim the title "'*Queen*' of Rock 'n' Roll" was wearing an immaculate white suit with sequins sewn into the lapels, a diamond-encrusted collar around his neck, extravagant rings and his trademark pompadour, and told him:

> I have taken this beauty all over the world. I have taken it to places where people didn't even think it was beautiful," said Little Richard. "One man told me: 'Go back to Africa where you came from.' I said, 'Africa? Who told you I was from Africa? I'm from Macon, Georgia. I am a peach.' But I was washing dishes at the Greyhound bus station in Macon, Georgia. Can you imagine? Beautiful hands like these...?[44]

This was quintessential Little Richard humor, a comic patina that more than likely covered up deep, indescribable pain and hurt.

But then pain tends to be the place out of which great artistry originates.

Three

A Dream Realized

THe year was 1955 and it had been three years since Little Richard took definitive steps toward a relationship with a recording studio that would finally pay off. He was now 22 and still a broke child of God scrubbing dishes in that same Greyhound bus station kitchen in Georgia.

He had managed to get a contract with Peacock Records where he recorded two singles backed by the Johnny Otis Trio. One of them, *"Little Richard's Boogie"* offered a glimpse of his expanding style. Then he cut a second group of recordings in 1954—*Directly From My Heart; Fool At The Wheel;* and *Red Beans, Rice and Turnip Greens*—even though many of these weren't issued until after Richard hit it big later with on Specialty Records.

When I first came out, there was no rock & roll.
There was swing and sway with Sammy Kaye. I
couldn't swing and I couldn't sway, so I had to boogie. They were singing *'Pennies from Heaven,'* but
the pennies weren't falling over my neighborhood.
My mother had 12 kids, and I had to do something
to help out my family. So I put blues and boogie-
woogie together and made rock 'n' roll. I'm the architect of rock 'n' roll; I created it.[45]

The label sent Richard out on the "Chittlin' Circuit" for
most of his dates. Richard had hoped he was finished
with those venues—mostly dives and juke joints up and
down the eastern seaboard across the north and through
the rust belt as far as Chicago.

The Chittlin' Circuit was the life blood and roots for
most black entertainers from the 1920s until the 1960s.
The venues were the safest places to play for musicians
of and audiences color in a time of abject discrimination
and race prejudice. Some venues, however, were larger
and attracted huge crowds of black folks. Places like the
Apollo, in Harlem, the Regal in Chicago, and the Fox in
Detroit paid well enough for a black performer to eek out
a living and were the most sought after. Once a black artist had worked his or her way up the food chain of popularity and success they could be booked into cross-over
venues like the Brooklyn Paramount in New York.

But Richard wasn't booked into these clubs and when
his records did not sell well, he found himself back in

Macon in the bus station kitchen, having failed again and licking his wounds.

To pass the time, he'd make up little song ditties, *Golly Miss Molly, and Tutti Fruitti,* as he washed the slop from plates. He sang into the greasy kitchen sink reimagining himself, determining that no matter what, his time would come. God would make it alright. They would all know him. He would find a way to explode into showbiz and illuminate the world. This dishwashing bus boy had a power and talent. He knew it—and it was growing quietly in that kitchen.

Richard decided that his destiny was not with the drag shows or the rural blues and Chitlin' Circuit. He was destined for the moon and elsewhere—television, radio, movies—and the deepest consciousness of America. Perhaps even the world. Then he saw an advertisement in the local newspaper that would change his life.

Singer Lloyd Price, who had a big hit on the R&B charts that year with *Lawdy, Miss Clawdy,* was coming to Macon to perform at the Macon City Auditorium. Richard started to think. Perhaps Price could steer him in the direction of someone who could help him get a record deal somewhere. Richard had nothing to lose by asking.

The following Friday, Richard went to the stage door of the Macon City Auditorium and waited. When Lloyd Price finally showed up Richard did almost the same thing he did with Sister Rosetta Tharpe years earlier—he ambushed him and asked for help by singing a cappella. Said Richard,

> Lloyd Price came through my hometown. He had this black-and-gold Cadillac, and I wanted a car like that. I said, "How'd you get famous?" He told me about Specialty and gave me the address.[46]

Price suggested Richard send a demo to Art Rupe, his friend at Specialty Records in Los Angeles. Richard thanked Price who thereafter became a good friend and he sent a hastily prepared package to Specialty without having been previously introduced to Art Rupe by Lloyd Price.

Specialty Records had been founded in 1944 by Rupe which was then called Jukebox Records. In 1946 he cashed in on the burgeoning "Race" music market with a huge hit, Roy Milton's *R.M. Blues.* Rupe personally produced many classic Blues and gospel recordings in Los Angeles, and had enjoyed ten years of moderate success re-

Art Rupe in 1953

cording black gospel and R&B. War-related industries had attracted an estimated two million working people to California from the southern states—a large majority of them black—and they found plenty of work and a new level of affluence which created a big demand for musical entertainment both live and on record. But black folks, who were still unwelcome in white theaters and clubs, wanted black music, not the white artists and records produced by the major record companies. Rupe, by 1955, was faced with a rapidly changing music and social scene and had no idea where he and his label should head.

With no musical training himself, save for an instinct he picked up from listening to records, Rupe placed control of Specialty's musical policy in the hands of Robert "Bumps" Blackwell who became Specialty's A&R man. It was an inspired move that made the company millions of dollars over the next two or three years.

On February 17, 1955, a raggedy tape box arrived at Specialty Records' office then located at 8508 Sunset Boulevard in Hollywood, California. It was just another tape from the umpteenth "dreamers and wanna-be's" perched atop the reception desk that showed up every week. The singer on the tape gave his own introduction: *"Mr. Art Rupe, you are now going to hear Little Richard and his Upsetters."*

Bumps Blackwell was the man whose job it was to listen to these potential dreams. He was a handsome, educated, 35-year-old black musician who joined Specialty following a distinguished musical career in his home city,

Seattle, Washington. There, he had nurtured and taught such emerging virtuosi's as Ray Charles and Quincy Jones. Blackwell said that "One day a reel of tape, wrapped in a piece of paper looking as though someone had eaten off it, came across my desk."[47] Blackwell gave it to Art Rupe. Remembers Rupe:

> Bumps Blackwell had just been hired about a week or two prior to that and his job was to listen to all the tapes... I can't say for certain whether he listened to the Little Richard tape or not, but the reason that we listened to it a second time was that Richard kept calling and bothering us. He was calling practically every other day... We both listened to [the tape] together. I made the decision that Richard did not sound like B.B. King but he had the same feeling and that, coupled with a gospel sound and a little more energy, was the basis for us being interested and deciding to sign him.[48]

Rupe was sufficiently impressed by Richard's demo that he called his Atlanta distributor, Paul Glass of All-state. Rupe then prepared for recording sessions in early March 1955.

Then came a problem: It was discovered that Richard was still under contract to Don Robey's Peacock label. Now Rupe had to figure out what to do. Richard, meanwhile, kept calling every week or so trying to get updates.

Two things happened to Richard between the time he sent those demos and the time Rupe got back to him: First, he met another southerner in Macon with a great voice and stage presence named James Brown. Brown was a year younger and earlier in 1955 contacted Little Richard while performing in a Macon club.

Richard, who had a generous sense of "pay it forward," to help artists like he himself had been helped, convinced the group to contact his then manager, Clint Brantley. Brantley agreed to manage Brown and The Flames and sent them to a local radio station to record a demo. They performed their own composition *Please, Please, Please*, which was inspired by Little Richard who wrote the words of the title on a napkin and gave it to Brown who became determined to make a song from it.

The song was a success and in March 1956 it became Brown's first R&B hit, selling over a million copies.[49] Despite their similar outrageous styles and slight competitiveness, the Godfather of Soul and the Architect of Rock & Roll remained dear friends until Brown's death in 2006.

The second thing to happen to Richard during his wait to hear from Rupe was much more damaging.

> I got into trouble with the law and had to stop appearing in Macon clubs," said Penniman. "There was this lady by the name of Fanny. I used to drive her around so I could watch people having sex with her. She'd be in the back of the car, the lights on, her legs open, and no panties on. ...She did it because I wanted her to do it. Well, I got put in jail for it. ...[T]he gas station man reported me to the police. ...Lewd conduct, they called it. My mother got a

lawyer. They took me before the judge and Lawyer Jacob said, 'This nigger here is going to leave town and he ain't ever coming back.' 'They're right your honor,' I replied. 'I'm leaving here and I'm not coming back here no more.' So they let me go, and I left Macon. I couldn't go back and play there no more because of that.[50]

In fact, Little Richard did not return to Macon for another decade.

In any event, that September 1955, months after he received Richard's demo tape, Rupe finally made contact and responded favorably. But he was frank about Richard's need to extricate himself from his contract with Robey and Peacock first. He told Richard that although he believed Richard had the appropriately "churchy" voice with which to compete with Atlantic Records and their up-and-coming blues star, Ray Charles, Richard would have to pay to get out of his contract with Peacock.

Naturally, Richard did not have the resources, so Rupe made the deal for Richard and paid $600 to buy out Richard's contract. It was a loan, of course. Then Rupe signed Little Richard to a contract with Specialty Records.

A series of short-term sessions was set up, thanks to Bumps, to give Richard a chance, much in the same way RCA had offered him a shot.

Richard remembers they called him early in the morning saying, "Meet us in New Orleans at J&M Studio."

They wanted him to record a couple of tunes. Richard's band had been playing in Fayetteville, Tennessee at the time. But J&M Studio was in New Orleans. Richard had to get there from Tennessee somehow.

> Me an' three of my band members loaded up the car and drove to New Orleans. As we were crossing Lake Pontchartrain Bridge it was raining so hard that we couldn't see to drive. The wipers on my old Chrysler weren't working, so we took coat hangers and tied them to the blades and worked them by hand so the driver could see the road.[51]

Finally. they got there. J&M Studio, located in the back of an appliance store on the corner of Rampart Street and Dumaine near the historic Congo Square, was a venue founded by Cosimo Matassa a decade earlier.

Matassa, one of the legendary recording engineers in the early era of rock, had hoped to tap into the rich pool of local talent, and within a couple years the studio was attracting interest from independent labels across the country. J&M hit its stride in 1949 with the first of several hits by local talent Fats Domino, and by the mid-1950s also developed a successful relationship with Specialty Records and Art Rupe through their singers Lloyd Price and Guitar Slim.

Rupe's right-hand guy, Bumps Blackwell was given the responsibility of meeting Little Richard and recording the sessions which included the Crescent City Rhythm Section, a band whose lineage carried a prestigious name in the jazz history of New Orleans. In addition to the search for a foil to neutralize Ray Charles and get a leg up against the competition, Rupe was also searching for a "piano-pounding man" to support one of his groups in New Orleans.

When Richard showed up at the Studio on September 13, 1955, with his weird look, garish clothes and hyper manner, the crew of veteran musicians thought he was a "kook."

"He walked into J&M like he was coming off stage. All that thick, thick powder makeup and the eyeliner and the lipstick and the hair everywhere in big, big waves," recalled drummer Earl Palmer. "Walked in there like something you'd never seen. I don't remember exactly what I said, but it was something like what the fuck is this, not who, what."

All the musicians reticence had a lot to do with Richards sexual flamboyance. "At that time everybody was a little concerned about being seen with somebody that looked and acted so gay," said Palmer.

But it wasn't long before Richard's fun loving personality had won them over. "Richard was so infectious and so unhiding with his flamboyancy, he sucked us right in," said Palmer. "We got to laughing with him instead of at him."

Blackwell found the wild-dressing, wild-talking man with his hair waved up half a foot to be exciting visually, but the vocals Richard delivered on those first tracks were lackluster. Blackwell was worried. It appeared as though another opportunity would go the way of the RCA

Robert "Bumps" Blackwell

deal for Richard and he would probably not last through the first session. Blackwell thought the vocals were too mild, especially for a guy whose stage act was famously outlandish and untamed. "If you look like Tarzan and sound like Mickey Mouse it just doesn't work out," Blackwell later explained.

He called for a break. As luck would have it, they took it at the local Dewdrop Inn on LaSalle Street. While Richard may not have experienced a great deal of time in important studios, a "club" like the Dewdrop Inn was definitely in his wheelhouse.

Impulsively, as a way of breaking the tension of the day's work, Richard started hamming it up for the daytime drunks, boosters, pimps, and whores hanging around. He jumped to the stage and began to pound away at the antique piano, screaming and hollering slightly obscene ditties filled with outrageous vocal effects, a show of physical histrionics, and a belligerent style of singing without any care for decorum. Richard sang his raunchy ode to sodomy that he used to play at dodgier clubs on the chittlin' circuit—a treatise to homosexuality called: *Tutti Fruitti...*"*A wop bop a loo mop / A good goddamn / Tutti Frutti / Good booty / If it don't fit/ Don't force it/ You can grease it / Make it easy.*"

Blackwell shook his head, "All you gotta do is give Richard an audience" as he sat there dumbfounded. But he responded immediately, "And *a good god-damn?*" he thought. "Now *that* is what I need to get on record. Wow! "That...is a hit!" he told Richard.

But Blackwell also knew that to navigate the record-ing through the rocky shoals of censorship, marketing and radio airplay, the lyrics had to be cleaned-up and family friendly, but the energy remain in Richard's powerful vocal performance.

He quickly called in a local songwriter he knew, Dorothy LaBostrie, to sanitize and write some new lyr-ics. "Good booty" became "aw rutti," and then there was a girl named Sue and a gal named Daisy. La-Bostrie delivered the words. Now armed with the new lyrics, they had almost run out of studio time. "In 15 minutes, we did two cuts. It has been history ever since," said Blackwell. [52]

The song was sensational. This was the Little Rich-ard who used to bang on cans and wail as a boy. Then and there he transformed into the Little Richard we know today. He was playing like crazy, singing loud, lewd, and hamming it up. Said Richard:

> I was really desperate and determined. I wanted to make it an help my family he said I was singing at the top of my voice. I was screaming. You never seen a guy with a big head like me scream as loud as I was hollering. I was screaming even louder than a holler. I screamed and played and banged the piano I almost tore that piano off the wall.

Drummer Earl Palmer observed,

> What I remember about those sessions is how physical they were. ...[O]ne reason I started playing what they have come to call a rock and roll beat. It came from trying to match Richard's right hand.

Dr. John, a New Orleans singer/song-writer was standing right outside J&M Studio when Richard was cutting *Tutti Frutti*. He commented that:

> Some people say Little Richard bummed his act from Esquerita. But to me S.Q., was more gospel sounding, and Richard was straight up hip. Richard was a totally original cat. Everything about him was off the hook.[53]

But all Richard wanted to do was impress and get

his career going in a lasting way. He became oblivious
to the reality that his performance style—wild, frenzied, and unrestrained—would transform him into
one of the most famous figures in the history of rock
and roll—and the song into one of the top 100 records
to change the world.

Four

Tutti Fruitti

Tutti Fruitt was released in November 1955 and became an overnight sensation. Little Richard instantly became the star we know him to be now— the Little Richard whose later protege, Jimi Hendrix, would say that he wanted to do with his guitar what Richard did with his voice.

This was the freakish, circus showman, the vamp, the diva. The Holy Ghost. He sounded breathless, fierce, and perhaps even a little unhinged. He was like the last man on earth singing the first song ever written. The reworked bubblegum lyrics did nothing to change the sexual urgency of the song, nor did Richard's vocal performance contain the fury or fun. Richard delivered it like a possessed preacher rapturously speaking in tongues. People didn't know what to make of it. Young folks bought the record like crazy—especially white kids. *Tutti Frutti* became an unqualified hit rising to #2 on the Billboard R&B chart in 1956. Fans, especially women, swarm the stage door for Little Richard. Once it was released, the song sold 200,000 copies in a week and a half. It would go on to spend 22 weeks on the R&B chart, reach #17 on the pop chart and, by 1968, sell over three million copies.

Richard was immediately sent on a nation-wide tour which climaxed with an appearance at Harlem's famed Apollo Theater with Guitar Slim. Art Rupe wanted Richard back in the J&M Studio where he knew the *Tutti Fruitti* formula could be repeated. He definitely wanted to cut a definitive version of *Slippin' And A'Slidin'* and *The Thing* (the original name of *Long Tall Sally*).

But while *Tutti Fruitti* was climbing the R&B charts, two white artists, Pat Boone and Elvis Presley covered it. Presley in particular had already covered other black singer's songs and made them hits, while the black singers had to make due with shorted, deficient sales coming only from their own community.

Since established record executives feared the economic consequences of the new popular music that they did not control because they were outdistanced by new, independent labels that had almost a monopoly on rock & roll acts by 1955, they worried about their share of the market, especially when white teens started to buy rock & roll records en masse.

To reverse this trend, larger companies signed white artists to copy or "cover" songs by African American artists, sometimes even sanitizing the lyrics. Charles "Pat" Boone, a descendent of pioneer Daniel Boone, became the most successful cover artist of the era. He wore white sweaters and white buck shoes, attended college, and idolized Bing Crosby. The singer, though speaking out against racism, refused "to do anything that will offend anybody. If I have to do that to be popular, I would rather not be an entertainer. I would rather not have a voice."

Couple this with the introduction of the 45-rpm record by the major companies, and it all helped undermine the power of the independents. Leon Rene of the small Exclusive Records outlined the effects of the new format:

> We had things going our way until [RCA] Victor introduced the 7-inch vinyl, 45-rpm record, which revolutionized the record business and made breakable, 10-inch 78-rpm obsolete overnight. We had to reduce the price of R&B records from a $1.05 to 75 cents, retail. This forced many independent companies out of business.

The new 7-inch records by 1956, accounted for $70 million in sales, mostly to teenagers who preferred the less breakable and the more affordable record. Two years later, the 45-rpm disc accounted for nearly 66 percent of all vinyl sales, the classical-music friendly 33 1/3 rpm grabbed 24 percent, and the heavy, breakable 78 rpm had fallen to less than 5 percent.

Through all of these efforts, businesspeople at the head of the major record companies suppressed or at least curtailed the success of the independents and their African American performers from two angles.

In September 1955, Boone hit the top of the charts with a cover of Fats Domino's *Ain't That a Shame*. He continued to score hits in the next two years with other covers such as *At My Front Door* by the El Dorados, Big Joe Turner's *Chains of Love*, and then Richard's *Tutti Fruitti*.

Whites covering black music in those days was a cruel burglary of original black content. But so captivating was the rhythmic drive of *Tutti Fruitti,* that when straight-laced Pat Boone sang it for a performance on Hit Parade, his recording of it outperformed Little Richard's recording going on to number #1 on the Pop charts—a feat which astonished and, frankly, angered Richard.

Blackwell said, "the white radio stations wouldn't play Richard's version of *Tutti Frutti* at first which made Boone's cover number one."[54] Said Richard:

...I was disgusted. Pat Boone's version sold more than I did. White families said I was demonic. They wanted a white role model for their kids, with white buck shoes on. So here come Pat Boone from Tennessee like he was a saint.[55]

Richard would go on to explain that parents of white kids didn't want him in the house, but that he got in anyway on the back of Pat Boone, as American households favored a model so much more like themselves. And even though Richard had already captured the young audience, he was sickened by Boone's version becoming a bigger Pop music hit. While it took a moment for the singer to finally take it all in good humor, Richard couldn't help but poke fun in one televised interview.

He imitated Boone's prim and proper voice singing *Fruitti*.... before interrupting it with his own version to illustrate

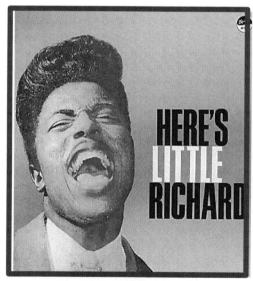

The fabulous Little Richard.
Permission by Concord Music Group, Inc.

the superior energy and performance in the original rendition. This would become an upsetting recurrent theme throughout Little Richard's career, as many white artists "covered" his music and achieved greater financial success with the white version of his songs, despite it sounding bland.

This was because before being called 'Rock & Roll,' Little Richard and other musicians produced what were called "Race" records—a category of music that marketed African American artists to African American audiences. But Little Richard's passion to perform and record music for anyone, regardless of skin color, generated wider interest and popularity for black music amongst white teenagers and white musicians.

Alas, as is always the case where cash is concerned, a big controversy arose once *"Fruitti..."* became an unqualified, international hit. Dorothy LaBostrie began telling people *she* wrote *"Tutti Fruitti,"* and that Little Richard had nothing to do with the writing of the song. Her version of the song's genesis is striking and worth mentioning whether you believe it or not. In his book *"I Hear You Knockin',"* Jeff Hannusch interviewed LaBostrie in 1985 (she died in 2007) and got this story:

> *I was listening to the radio and an announcement came on that immediately caught my attention. It said that Bumps Blackwell was looking for songwriters. Well, as soon as I heard where he was gonna be, I decided I was gonna be a songwriter. I was working as a cook for a lady and I told her that I had to quit because I was going to write a hit record. She probably thought I was crazy, but that's exactly what I did. I practically broke*

Cosimo's door down the next day. Little Richard was sitting at the piano and it was the first time I'd ever laid eyes on him. I just asked to hear his voice and I sat down and put 'Tutti Frutti' down on paper in 15 minutes.

...Little Richard didn't write none of 'Tutti Frutti'. I'll tell you exactly how I came to write that. I used to live on Galvez Street, and my girlfriend and I liked to go down to the drug store and buy ice cream. One day we went in and saw this new flavor, Tutti Frutti. Right away I thought, 'Boy, that's a great idea for a song.' So I kept it in the back of my mind until I got to the studio that day."[56]

LaBostrie also gave an interview to *Open Vault from WGBH,* and this was her answer when asked "How did *Tutti Frutti* get started, and wasn't Little Richard singing a lot of songs with nasty lyrics?"

LaBostrie replied:

Dorothy LaBostrie in 1958

Yes, nasty, nasty, nasty... He would sing dirty blues that would make your hair curl and I couldn't take it."
"...In 15 minutes I sat down and wrote "Tutti Frutti" in the corner. I asked him [Little Richard] what he'd like. I listened to his voice and I sat down and I wrote it. In other words, I already had the title of it because when

my girlfriend and I went to the drugstore and I wanted vanilla ice cream, she said, they got a new one. So I said tutti frutti, I said oh rootie, I said, oh, I got a song. And I throwed it on in back in my mind.

But when the time came and I went to the studio, I went into the room by myself in a corner and I wrote "Tutti Frutti" when I came back out and he stood at the piano, he never sat down to play, never, not that I've ever seen him sit down. He went to banging, banging, hollering and then I took the song up and be-gan to sing - wamp poma luma poma lump, bam boom, tutti frutti... And when I come to find out they said two or three people had written "Tutti Frutti." I said they couldn't. But then Art Rupe, when Cosimo had called him 'cause they had told Cosimo that I didn't write it. And Cosimo was the one that calls me today to be where I'm at, Cosimo called Art Rupe in California and Art Rupe got in touch with me and my mother had had a stroke... he said, you need some money? He said I heard you wrote that song I listened to. I said, yes, I said. 'How much money would you want?' And I thought 50 dollars was a whole lot of money. I said, I could use 50 dollars. 'No, he say, you look for 500 dollars in the morning and he sent me 500 dollars and the next week he sent another 500 when he sent me the big check I got two thousand four hundred fifty-four dollars and seventy-eight cents. That was my first big check that I got from "Tutti Frutti".[57]

Phil Walden, who went on to manage Otis Redding

and found Capricorn Records, recalled his first encounter with Little Richard at the Macon City Auditorium:

> Little Richard just destroyed me. He was doing a lot of the songs that he later recorded, but off-color, like *'Tutti Frutti.' 'Tutti frutti / Good booty / Miss Lucy is juicy / Miss Tight is all right / It ain't the ocean, it's the motion...'* oh, all kinds of things. And he would wave to all the gay guys, all his 'sisters' in the audience.[58]

As for the *"Awop Bop Aloo Mop"* that begins the song, Richard told a Rolling Stone interviewer in the late 1960s:

> I was working at the Greyhound Bus Station in Macon, Georgia, oh my Lord, back in 1955. ... I was washing dishes ... at the time. I couldn't talk back to my boss man. He would bring all these pots back for me to wash, and one day I said, 'I've got to do something to stop this man bringing back all these pots back to me to wash, and I said, 'Awop bop aloo bop a wop bam boom, take 'em out!' and that's what I meant at the time." Richard said he also wrote "Good Golly, Miss Molly" and "Long Tall Sally" in that Greyhound Bus Station kitchen.[59]

Additionally, when Cosimo Matassa, who owned J&B Studio where the hit was recorded, was asked about it by writer David Kirby, he agreed with both Blackwell and LaBostrie's versions. Blackwell had said Dorothy cleaned up Little Richard's raunchy lyrics, and LaBostrie said she was writing about ice cream. "Who's telling the truth?" asked Kirby. "Both!" said Matassa.

> You have to understand, Dorothy's a nice lady, but she gives herself more credit than she should. ...'Tutti Frutti' was a club song with no real end; a guy with a blue suit might walk in, and you'd put in a verse about a guy in a blue suit. So it was whatever Little Richard wanted it to be at the moment, and at that moment, it was dirty.[60]

Whether you believe Blackwell, Matassa, or La-Bostrie, my advice is to take LaBostrie's story with a "wink and a nod." Reality suggests that after the mega-success of *Tutti Frutti*, one would have expected Specialty Records (or others) to beat down Labostrie's door for more songs and/or material. But except for contributing to the rousing, *Rich Woman* for Li'l Millet, that was not the case, and no one is alive to refute her story except Richard who isn't talking.

I believe memories are always subject to enhanced interpretation when money and ego are involved. Miss LaBostrie was given co-songwriter credit for the song and I would not discount Bumps Blackwell's story which Richard has had more than 60 years to refute. All we know is the record sold over a million copies after its release, and for Little Richard it succeeded in building strong ties to an audience that included hordes of white as well as black kids.

Frankly, that became the true measure of the song—its impact—which went far beyond its sales. An impact which was responsible for and urged on nonviolent integration through music and dance in much the same way as Dr. Martin Luther King's speech at the Montgomery Improvement Association meeting to end discrimination on the public bus system did in Alabama when Rosa Parks refused to give her seat to a white man the same month *Tutti Fruitti* was released. Said Dr. King: *"...[T]here comes a time when people get tired of being trampled over by the iron feet of oppression... The only weapon that we have in our hands this evening is the weapon of protest."*

Said Little Richard using his own weapon of protest:

"She rock to the East, she rock to the West, She is the gal that I love best, Tutti frutti, aw rootie, Tutti frutti, aw rootie, Tutti frutti, aw rootie, Awop bop aloo mop alop bam boom!"

'Nuff said.

Little Richard had taken America by storm. If audiences had never heard anything like Little Richard before, they certainly hadn't seen anything like him either. From his mainstream debut, Richard's look was singular: pencil thin moustache, an outrageous pompadour, face make-up and an equally outlandish wardrobe. Richard was "Out there," a complete, flamboyant original like nothing anyone ever experienced on stage—a guru to young people. His over-the-top performance style and androgynous persona would later help lay the framework for future rock gender-benders like Mick Jagger, David Bowie, Michael Jackson, and Prince.

The demand for personal appearances, even in southern states, began eroding the taboos against black artists appearing in white clubs and dance halls. Everyone wanted to see the creator of this new sound which Alan Freed the disc-jockey icon coined "Rock 'n' Roll," and his act was an experience. Richard recalled:

> We were breaking through the racial barrier. The white kids had to hide my records 'cos they daren't let their parents know they had them in the house. We decided that my image should be crazy and way-out so that the adults would think I was harmless.[61]

But however eccentric and fun he was, even Little Richard had his critics. In fact, Richard's look and sound were far too radical for many mainstream (read: white) audiences. Some targeted him for the simple fact he was a black gay man. Being a homosexual performer was almost unheard of at the time. But being *black* and homosexual was as rare and non-existent as it came.

Many people did not approve of the album's hit song, *Tutti Frutti*. For many, the word "Frutti" (or "fruity") was another word for "gay" which at the time was disap-proved of. There were so many homophobic people who were disheartened by the song and its use of the word that they refused to tolerate Little Richard. This led to quite a few of Richard's concerts being banned—some-times due to white supremacist laws in the south. The concerts were also banned for being integrated and an interracial mixing ground. These concerts were seen as being "associated with rebellion." But rebellious it was.

African-American music of the late-blues, early-rock period was already alien enough to middle-class, white American families, but when it was transformed into this aggressive variation as articulated by Little Richard, it became one of the young music genre's first big cultural affronts. To traditionalists, rock—particularly in this ra-cially charged form—was an invasion; and to rock devo-tees, the "*un*-cool," "squares," just didn't get it.

With the entrance of Elvis Presley's physical gyrations and Little Richard's screaming, piano-pounding, offen-sive texts, the "*un*-cool" could no longer hold back the surrender of a fascinated young national audience.

Battle lines were drawn between the generations. White parents would look up in bewilderment when they heard Richard screeching, "*Awop-bop-aloo-mop*," then watched in horror as their teenagers rushed to dance with each other. That is where integration and real race-mixing—the very thing many whites were terrified of—

was occurring: on the dance floor, not just in the music. The races came together there where all inhibitions were flung to the four winds and an exuberance of primal ecstasy took over.

In his biography of Fats Domino, Rick Coleman, relays a sample of thwarted parental desire for suppression of white teenage euphoria with Rock & Roll music: In a 1956 show in Houston, blacks were allowed to dance but not with whites. But when white teenagers hit the dance floor, it was decided that only whites could dance. Outspoken Fats Domino declared, "I won't play if Negroes can't dance." Though teens of every color began to boogie together, police stopped the show, provoking a riot.[62]

It was the same with Little Richard's music. In Baltimore, Richard's band became flummoxed when white girls threw panties on the stage. By the end of the night everyone was mixed up together dancing. It may have started out segregated, but it never ended that way. Young people couldn't sit down. They *had* to dance—and it didn't matter to white kids if the one they danced with did *not* look like them. Said Richard:

> *Tutti Frutti* really started the races being together. When I was a boy, white people would sit upstairs. They called it 'white spectators,' and the blacks was downstairs, and white kids would jump over the balcony and come down where I was and dance with the blacks. We started that merging all across the country. From the git-go, my music was accepted by whites.[63]

Notwithstanding, while Rock & Roll did bring the races together, there was always an undercurrent of violence attached to the genre that was racist in origin. In February 1956, shortly after Richard's appearance at the Apollo in Harlem, a black boy was shot in the ankle by a white fan at a Rock & Roll dance in New York, suggesting that there was no simple or necessary correlation between love for the same music and racial goodwill.

Then, to Richard's point above, less than three months later, on May 4, 1956, there was a major race riot at the American Legion Auditorium in Roanoke, Virginia, where a revue featuring Little Richard, the Cadillacs, Ruth Brown and Fats Domino was playing.

As was customary for "black" entertainers who attracted white customers, the Legion's segregation laws were observed by allocating the balcony to white patrons while blacks occupied the main floor. However, more than 2,000 whites tried to cram into the allotted balcony which barely had space for half that number. Some sought to escape the crush by moving down to the main floor where eventually they were spotted "actually dancing" with black folks—as one paper noted. As the three hour show concluded, some whites incensed by the violation of Jim Crow laws, or perhaps being drunk, began hurling whisky bottles at the black crowd below. Three dozen on and off duty policemen broke up the riot, and six people including two black patrons, were eventually charged and convicted of disorder and resisting arrest.[64]

Scenes like this were evident throughout the South,

and Little Richard, in '56 and '57, was forced to take it in stride—if he was to survive and be successful. But it was hard on his psyche.

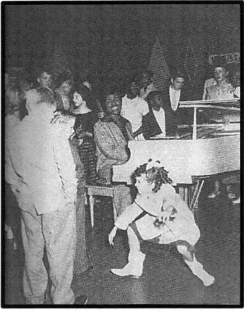

In the end, however, it was the music, and the music could not be denied. Not by blacks. Not by whites. With *Tutti Frutti*, Little Richard was demanding full citizenship in a society that only granted it

Little Richard and a young girl enjoying "Tutti Fruitti" with a racially mixed crowd in 1956

to him provided he stayed out of sight.

But he didn't. Richard was an out-front-and-center talent with all the outrage and fury of a combustible generation exploding with change.

Often, I wonder what the Rock & Roll music scene would look like if Richard's initial recordings at J&M Studio hadn't been sufficiently bland enough for Bumps Blackwell to stop the session and call for a break; and that Richard hadn't jumped onto that piano at the Dew Drop Inn and launched into his raunchy rendition of *Tutti Fruitti*.

But thank God he did…for music history's sake.

Five

Long Tall Richard — The Georgia Peach

Right after his appearance at the Apollo, in early 1956, Richard signed with Bumps Blackwell to manage him. Together they co-wrote Richard's next single, *Long Tall Sally* along with a young 16 year old girl named Enortis Johnson. There is a great account regarding how the song came about—the stuff of legend.

Bumps tells the story that after what had happened initially with white radio stations not wanting to play Richard's *Tutti Fruitti* in favor of Pat Boone's, he and Richard wanted to make it more difficult for white artists to attempt to recreate the Little Richard magic and top the charts before Richard could.

They decided their next single would have faster-paced lyrics that Pat Boone couldn't replicate. Around this time, popular DJ Honey Chile introduced Bumps to Enortis. She had parts of the initial lyrics for a song for

Richard to record to raise money for an operation needed by her Aunt Mary. Said, Blackwell:

> I went along to this awful downtown hotel, and there was Honey Chile with this young girl, about sixteen, seventeen, with plaits, all white starched collars and everything. So Honey Chile said to me, 'Bumps, you got to do something about this girl. She's walked all the way from Opelousas, Mississippi, to sell this song to Richard, 'cos her auntie's sick and she needs money to put her in the hospital.' I said 'okay, let's hear the song', and this little clean-cut kid says, 'Well, I don't have a melody yet. I thought maybe you or Richard could do that.' So I said okay, what have you got.
>
> She pulls out this piece of paper. It looked like toilet paper with a few words written on it: *'Saw Uncle John with Long Tall Sally. They saw Aunt Mary comin', So they ducked back in the alley.* And she said, 'Aunt Mary is sick. And I'm going to tell her about Uncle John. 'Cos he was out there with Long Tall Sally, and I saw 'em. They saw Aunt Mary comin' and they ducked back in the alley.'[65]

Not wanting to upset an influential DJ, Bumps took the "song" to Richard. They decided, after experimenting with the lyrics, that the phrasing could be sung fast which would suit their purposes. Between Robert and Richard, they finished the song and recorded it for their follow-up single. Said Blackwell, "We decided to up the tempo on the song and have the lyrics go so fast Boone wouldn't be able to get his mouth together to do it!"[66]

Though the working titles used for the song included *The Thing* and *Bald Headed Sally,* they went with *Long Tall Sally,* and it was an explosive follow-up to *Tutti Fruitti.*

The song was released in February 1956 and it became one of the great double-sided hits of the era. *Long Tall Sally,* climbed even higher on the charts and was Little Richard's biggest and highest ranking hit he ever achieved. It scored #1 on the R&B charts, #6 hit on the Billboard pop charts, and #3 in Britain.

Its B-side single, *Slippin' and Slidin'* went to #2 on the R&B charts. Like its predecessor, *Tutti Fruitti,* the Specialty 45 ended up in both the Grammy and Rock & Roll Halls of Fame and help spread the word about the unique entertainer people came to know as the "Georgia Peach."

In fact, Richard's huge influence on The Beatles was due in no small part to this particular single, which they would demonstrate in later years.

The Beatles recorded *Long Tall Sally* as the lead track of their 1964 EP, and Paul McCartney performed it with his new group Wings on their 1972 UK college tour. The Liverpool idols also played *Slippin' and Slidin'* during their *Get Back* rehearsals, and John Lennon chose the song as part of his 1975 covers album *Rock 'n' Roll.*

Both songs have been covered endlessly, *Long Tall Sally* attracted versions by Elvis Presley, Eddie Cochran, the Kinks, and Jerry Lee Lewis to name a few. Aside from

Lennon, *Slidin'* was covered by Buddy Holly, Johnny Winter and Otis Redding and was so popular that it climbed to No. 33 in its own right, as Little Richard, one of rock 'n' roll's true originals, became a bigger star by the week.

What is hilarious is Richard and Blackwell's original intention for *Long Tall Sally* backfired. Pat Boone released his version of the song shortly after Richard's which peaked at #8 on the pop charts. In fact, *Long Tall Sally* was been covered by 136 artists as of this writing.

Richard went out on tour again, and soon a penchant for outrageous costumes followed. In addition to satin suits in loud colors, he was experimenting with rhinestones, brooches, sequins and glitter. If he became hot during a performance, he took off his jacket and threw it into the crowd who'd go riotous trying to catch it.

Art Rupe had Little Richard record a wealth of material in two recording sessions at J&M Studio in 1956 and 1957. Richard cut such tunes as *Long Tall Sally, Rip It Up, Good Golly Miss Molly, Whole Lotta Shakin' (Goin' On),* and *Lucille* amongst so many others. In fact, from the time he began with Specialty on September 13, 1955 until he left in October 1957, Little Richard recorded over fifty songs.

From this material Specialty released 9 singles and two albums. In fact, for those eighteen months everything Richard recorded was a hit and club dates were sellouts.

For Little Richard, *Tutti Frutti* started an uninter-rupted string of top 10 hits. He sang them all in sold-out concerts across America including: *Long Tall Sally, Rip It Up, Lucille,* and *Whole Lotta Shakin' (Goin' On).* He had done it. The dream he had while forced to wash dishes in that bus station had come true. He was the big-gest and brightest star in the world who was still ascend-ing. He gave extra-terrestrial sensations to white and black teenagers and opened up channels only subcon-sciously thought-out. He freaked out girls, he freaked out boys; he freaked out parents, priests, politicians, police, and anyone else watching his rise. No one could catch him. He stood up at his piano and destroyed the crowd by flashing his teeth, taking off his clothes, and becoming lightning in a bottle. His performances knitted freedom into our pleasure centers.

As the least boring person anyone ever saw, he almost felt dangerous, unknown—yet exciting, and he dimin-ished everything else around him. Little Richard was no one religion. He was *every* religion.

Now, with money coming in and his stardom securely in place, Richard did something he'd wanted to do all along. He moved his mother and siblings into a big house in Los Angeles on the west side. He also bought himself a gold 1956 Fleetwood Cadillac.

Little Richard had arrived.

When people started admiring me and my songs went gold I decided to buy a home in Hollywood and bring my family there to live. Art Rupe gave me ten thousand dollars to put down on a house at 1710 Virginia Road, in West L.A., the Sugar Hill district. The house cost twenty-five thousand dollars. It was next door to the world boxing champion, Joe Louis who was born and raised in Macon like me. But Art Rupe wasn't giving me nothing. He deducted it from my royalty checks. That's how it was. You made the hits, you sold the records, then when the royalty statements arrived you'd find you owed them.[67]

It was true. Richard was doing well, but not at the level his white counterparts were doing for the same effort—or many times with his same songs. It was because he was discovered young when all performers want to do is to have a record that gets on the radio, and people know their name. If you made enough for a house and a Cadillac, you were a star. Never mind the business end—royalties, mechanics rights, publishing rights, performance rights—all the things that Art Rupe knew about and cheated Richard out of like so many label owners did with unaware talent.

Once a performer discovered their true value, the cost of retrieving what a label might owe them was expensive with law firm fees. On top of this they would be past their competitive interest, or too old to have relevance in the industry anymore. The record label would just move on to some other unsuspecting young talent.

Specialty's deal with Richard was typical of the company's dealings with their artists. In the 1950s, the standard royalty received from record companies was five percent of ninety percent of the retail price of the record. In those days, a 45 sold for eighty-nine

Little Richard in his first Cadillac, 1956

cents. The performer could expect to receive four cents for each record sold, plus a broadcast fee, calculated on the number of airplays it received, which could be one or two cents. The song's publisher retained the "mechanical right" to the song, which meant that the record company paid out one cent for each of the songs on the record. If the songwriter nominated themselves as the publisher of the songs, they receive, in addition to any royalty and broadcast fees, two-cent mechanical fees on every copy sold.

Art Rupe owned the publishing company that bought Richard's songs. He leased them to his own recording company at one-half rate, which cut Richard's share of the mechanicals to half a cent. Says Richard:

> "I had signed a very bad deal with Specialty. If you wanted to record you signed on their terms or you didn't record. I got a half cent for every record sold. Whoever heard of cutting a penny in half!"[68]

It didn't matter how many records you sold if you were black. The publishing rights were sold to the record label before the record was released—and in this case, *Tutti Frutti* was sold to Specialty for $50.

Writer David Kirby saw a conversation between Little Richard, Chuck Berry and Bo Diddley in a 1987 Taylor Hackford documentary, *"Chuck Berry: Hail! Hail! Rock 'n' Roll!"* where the discussion between the legends went like this:

BO DIDDLEY: Money. ...You know, I sat up all night, looking at the contract, trying to figure out how I was going to make any money out of two, two...

CHUCK BERRY: Half a cent a record.

LITTLE RICHARD: Well, you had to sell two records to make a penny.

CHUCK BERRY: Now a record cost 59 cents; that means 58 cents was going somewhere else.

LITTLE RICHARD: Now I, I, I ... whoo, boy!

CHUCK BERRY: I majored in math. I was looking at the other 58 cents.

LITTLE RICHARD: I majored in mouth! I was doing all the talking and no walking. I couldn't even understand the contract. When I got it, all I wanted to see was "Little Richard." When I saw that, I thought, "Whoo — I've got a contract!"[69]

Later in the show Bo Diddley rightfully asserts "R&B don't stand for nothin' but rip-off and bullshit."[70] In other words, what Diddley, Chuck Berry and Little Richard were playing was 'Rock & Roll' until white folks started playing it. Then suddenly, it became 'Rhythm & Blues," which meant ghetto music. Another name for 'Race Music' thus prompting bad pay.

So, in order to make any real money groups had to go on the road. Not that concert promoters weren't as much thieves as labels, but at least the performer or their representative could approach the promoter after the gig and demand payment then and there versus waiting for a royalty statement that deducted everything and left you anticipating for months.

Nonetheless, Richard was making money. Not as much as Elvis or Jerry Lee Lewis or Pat Boone, but during those wild years of the fifties, Little Richard was earning more money than he could count. He would actually carry a suitcase on tour filled with cash. People around him were stealing left and right and Richard knew it, but he was having so much fun he didn't really care.

Soon, the IRS was after him to account for his earnings, and he began to tire of the lifestyle. The constant traveling and encounters with racism were getting to him.

The road is a lonely place and for most musicians there is a lure to find either stable romance, or random sex in every town. If a musician was married, perhaps they'd bring their spouse. Most times this was not possible because if children were involved, someone had to parent. Also it gets grueling for a spouse—night after night waiting backstage or at the hotel with little to do.

In Richard's case, the road did what it had done when he was even younger, it opened his appetite for more sexual exploration. Though he was homosexual, he also liked women on occasion which probably made him what we now call "sexually fluid" and it was women who threw themselves (and their panties) at him. At the stage door every night would be hordes of girls willing to do whatever it took to be with Richard just to tell friends or have the experience.

But for Richard there were also hordes of men. Black men, white men, big, small, and in-between men—and Richard had his fill. He would invite his sexual audience back to his hotel room—or in most cases several rooms—and after drinking and having a joint, be entertained. But Richard's preferred action was just watching—and masturbating. His voyeurism increased on that first tour and he would watch two or three women sexually go at each other or with several men while he watched and satisfied himself on the side.

In 1984, writer Charles White and Little Richard had lunch and White queried him outright: "...I have to ask about your sex life." Richard grinned and answered quickly, "Well, ...we are all both male and female. Sex to me is like a smorgasbord. Whatever I feel like, I go for. What kind of sexual am I? I'm omnisexual!'"[71]

But even with his new-found success—his new house, his car, his wild friends, and his money, something was still bothering him. Was it isolation? Loneliness? A need for genuine affection not based on his stardom and affected onstage look?

Perhaps.

But Richard did find one woman who captured his heart, his mind and his body—no matter how bizarre their relationship was throughout the decades. She befuddled, intoxicated, and excited Richard, and all he could do was to go with it for as long as nature allowed.

Buddy Holly and Little Richard, circa 1955

Six

Angel, Films and Angels

On June 8, 1956 while on tour in Savannah, Georgia, Richard was staring out of his hotel window when he saw a woman with the most sensational body he'd ever seen—one to make him scream, *"Good Golly, Miss Molly."*

Her name was Audrey Robinson and she was the biracial cousin of soul singer Solomon Burke. She had very light skin making her almost look white, a large bustline, small waist, and she was a college hopeful.

Sexually objectifying her (as men did be they straight or closeted gay in those days), would prove one of the most significant moments in Richard's sexual life—that first glimpse of the woman he would come to know as Lee Angel—an exotic dancer and stripper. She would become his favored accomplice at what would later be his orgies and "special parties."

Richard sent a band member down to get her.

I was just walking down West Broad Street, in Savannah," Lee Angel told journalist Jonny Whiteside in 2018, "and someone came up to me on the street and said, 'Excuse me, Little Richard wants to meet you,'" Sharing Richard's sense of irony she cracked, "'Does he know I'm a girl?' But curiosity

Audrey Robinson, nee *Lee Angel* , 1957

kicked in, and I walked in that room, took one look at Richard, and we're still close 68 years later.[72]

Lee Angel says she was captivated from the second she met Richard even though in her mind it all started as an out-of-nowhere fluke.

> I was not a fan. It was 1956, I was done with high school for the day and out doing an errand for my stepmom. All the kids were excited about the big dance that night with Little Richard, but they said, 'We know you won't be there,' because I hated Little Richard's music.

But clearly when she met the Rock & Roll star, things changed.

I almost fainted. I felt weak at the knees. I went through all the classic signs of falling in love. With Richard, I have had a lot of firsts.[73]

Little Richard remembered the event as if yesterday.

I saw this beautiful young girl with this fantastic body, fifty-inch bust and eighteen-inch waist. It's true that nothing grows in the shade! ...I asked one of my band men to go across the street and ask her to come over to the hotel. ...A few weeks later she turned up at a concert in Wilmington, Delaware. She had decided to come with me. When we left for Washington, D.C. that night Angel traveled with us in my car. We checked into the Hotel Dunbar, in Washington, and we shared a room. She was a wonderful lover.

...From the beginning she seemed to know exactly what I wanted in sex. She would do anything to excite me, including having sex with other guys while I watched. I loved Angel and Angel loved me, but in different ways. ...I loved Angel because she was pretty, and the fellers enjoyed having sex with her. She could draw a lot of handsome guys for me. She was like a magnet. She drew everything to me. You ain't never seen a woman made like Angel. ...She was some girl.[74]

The two hooked up immediately and an allegorical coupling began. For Richard she may have served as a "beard" especially given his bisexuality (at least then), and penchant for wild orgies.

Angel hit the road with Richard following him from city to city on his tour. She participated in most of Little Richard's legendary orgies and sex romps while on the road. The two were inseparable.

In Little Richard's own words, "Me and Angel one night were having a big orgy," said Richard. "We got naked. Me, Angel and three fellas smoked angel dust. We were crawling about on the floor like dogs, naked. We got dusty from the angel dust. We were afraid to answer the door. We were afraid to answer the phone."[75]

Angel was his 1950's groupie. A backstage asset who exerted an irresistible force over Little Richard, Screamin' Jay Hawkins and later Jackie Wilson. She was both a burlesque legend and the ultimate rock & roll insider. In fact, when John Lennon and Yoko Ono got together, Apple execs ponied up long coin and begged Angel to break them up—but she would have no part of the sleazy scheme, she has said.

A veteran voyeur by age 24 when he met Lee Angel, over 50 years later, then septuagenarian Little Richard told British GQ magazine in 2010 that Angel was his "life-long soul mate."[76]

Soon, motion pictures came calling for Richard with his success in records. Lee Angel was with him in Los Angeles as the offers were pouring in. After the box-office smash, *Rock Around the Clock*, starring Bill Haley and the Comets became a huge hit, Columbia Pictures wanted a follow-up to capitalize on teenagers cravings to see their favorite stars. The sequel was *Don't Knock the Rock*, which would again feature Bill Haley and the Comets. But it also showcased the legendary D.J. Alan Freed.

In September 1956, Little Richard and his band The Upsetters were back in Los Angeles filming a part for *Don't Knock The Rock* in black & white.

When the film was released audiences loved it. By all accounts, Little Richard—who sang *Tutti Frutti* and *Long Tall Sally*—somehow managed to steal the film from Bill Haley himself. The wild freedom of Little Richard's performance in the film changed the lives of hundreds of thousands of young people.

It was a box-office smash hit in the U.S., and after its release in Europe two years later it instigated riots in England, Germany, and Ireland.

Following his success in *Don't Knock the Rock*, Art Rupe had news for Richard about another major Rock & Roll film appearance. Twentieth Century Fox was planning an extravagant movie to be shot in color and in cinemascope. It would feature some of the top stars in the business: Jayne Mansfield, Tom Ewell and Edmond O'Brien would play the leads. It was tentatively entitled, *Do Re Mi* and Fox wanted Little Richard to be in the film. It was another dream come true for Richard.

Rupe had some new songs which could be used and

he was keen on getting some of these numbers cut while Richard was on the West Coast. On September 6, he took Richard and the Upsetters into Master Recorders where they worked on cuts of *I Got It* and *Send Me Some Lovin'*. The only classic to emerge from this session was *She's Got It* which was selected by Fox and released as a single in October 1956. It went to #15 on the Billboard charts. But Rupe was determined to have the title song in the film and the deadline for the movie, now retitled *The Girl Can't Help It*, was fast approaching. He still needed more material.

So he booked additional studio time at Cosimo Matassa's J&M Studio in New Orleans for October 15 and 16. He flew down personally to supervise the sessions —which did not sit well with Bumps Blackwell, Richard's manager. The first recording was *Jenny Jenny*, (with *Miss Ann* on the "B" side) which wasn't released until May 1957 and became Little Richard's fifth million seller.

But competition for the title song was now serious.

Fats Domino, who was topping the charts in October 1956 with his revival of the oldie Blueberry Hill, was in line to record the title song which had been especially commissioned for the film: *The Girl Can't Help It*.

Art Rupe had to think fast—and somehow he managed to persuade Twentieth Century Fox to give the title song to Little Richard instead.

Rupe flew to New Orleans to produce a session which included the song, *The Girl Can't Help It* on October 16th. The song had been written by veteran songwriter and jazz pianist Bobby Troup, the composer of route 66. Said Rupe: *"It wasn't written as a rock 'n' roll song. As a matter of fact Bobby Troup was shocked when he heard it."* [77]

On the same day, influenced by the success of Domino's Blueberry Hill, Rupe supervised Richard as he cut two oldies: *Baby Face* and *By The Light of The Silvery Moon*. But both of these songs, which were too radical a departure from Richard's established métier, stayed in the can.

The film *The Girl Can't Help It* was released in the U.S., on December 1, 1956. Richard's performance in it for which he indeed recorded the title track, was revelatory, and the film has been hailed as the best Rock & Roll movie ever.

The title song for *The Girl Can't Help It* was released a week later and it shot to #11 (R&B) and #49 on the Pop charts. It did even better in the U.K. where it went to #9.

But there was now a whole growing sector of the population who saw Rock & Roll music as a dangerous threat to the existing social paradigm—particularly racists and white supremacist groups in the South. They had begun putting out frank and inflammatory statements that sent tremors through America's establishment. The North Alabama White Citizens Council in particular, started a campaign against "Negro B-bop and rock & roll music."

The group attempted to persuade radio stations not to play those tunes and on April 10, 1956 three men apparently affiliated with the White Citizens Council attacked Black musician Nat King Cole who was preforming before an all white audience in the Birmingham Municipal Auditorium. The hate group then went on TV and declared: "Rock & Roll is part of a test to undermine the morals of the youth of our nation. It is sexualistic, unmoralistic and ...brings people of both races together."[78]

One circular distributed in the South read: "Notice! Stop! Help save the youth of America. Don't buy Negro records. If you don't want to serve Negroes in your place of business, then don't have Negro records on your jukebox or listen to Negro records on the radio. The screaming idiotic words and savage music of these records are undermining the morals of our white youth in America. Call the advertisers of radio stations that play this type of music and complain to them!"

But Richard had plans to be the biggest star in the world, black or white—and people would have to accept him—and his lifestyle.

During filming of movies, and his road shows, Lee Angel was ever at his side, performing her sexual or voyeuristic duties for Richard who had begun to drink and smoke marijuana more. The orgies continued. He had unknowingly pulled away from his family not seeing or contacting them for months at a time while on the road.

By the turn of 1957, Richard's touring schedule was exhausting. But it was also at its height thus making it difficult to get him into a studio. While he was back East Richard took his band The Upsetters into a Washington D.C., radio station where on January 16, 1957 he cut two of his most devastating rockers, *Keep A'Knockin'*, and *Ooh My Soul*. Even though Louis Jordan had cut a version of *Keep A'Knockin'* for Decca Records in 1939 Rupe released a spliced intercut of Richard's recording in August 1957. It made it to #5 (R&B) and #8 (Pop). It was Little Richard's sixth million seller.

Then one day while Richard was finally at home in Los Angeles, a religious advocate, Brother Wilbur Gulley knocked on Richard's door for the purpose of selling bibles. He and Richard began talking about religion, the Bible, church and soon they began associating on a regular basis. Their talks made Richard realize how much he missed singing in church and how good he felt to be connected to God when he did.

Then one morning, after waking up from an orgy somewhere in Houston, Texas, naked and not knowing where he was, he heard a voice say: "That's enough, Richard!" He didn't know if it was God or a guardian angel instructing him, but he threw everyone out of his room.

As the scrambling bodies grabbed their clothes mumbling and cursing him, Richard got his bible and read it.

This was the first of three major signs he received that year that he interpreted as "celestial" warnings.

The second sign occurred during his tour of Australia with singers Eddie Cochran and Gene Vincent.

On October 12, 1957, Richard was flying from Melbourne to Sydney sitting next to Bumps Blackwell when he suddenly saw something odd—a vision. Outside his window are four white angels, wings flapping, holding the plane up while it looked as though one of the engines was on fire. He showed Bumps. "Man, what is that?" But Bumps saw nothing out of the ordinary. Richard looked

again. The plane was normal.

In Melbourne, Richard grabbed headlines:

New Castle Morning Herald 1957-10-03
"Singer Dragged Over Footlights"

Screaming teenage admirers of an American Negro rock & roll exponent Little Richard, dragged him across the footlights and trampled him in a mob on the floor of Newcastle Stadium at the latest Big Show last night. Attendants had to remove an over- excited teen's foot from Little Richard's face before they could help him to his feet and rescue him from the mob.

Took Off Coat

Little Richard virtually invited himself to be dragged off the stage at the second performance of the show. He had been on stage only a few minutes before he peeled off the coat of a blue costume, akin to a pair of pajamas, he was wearing. "Singing" bare-chested in his pants, with the top of his underpants showing, and removing his red-and-white shoes, he appeared to tear small pieces from the coat and threw them into the audience.

Later, he threw a belt and gestured as though about to throw a ring and watch. When he quivered and rolled and dropped to the floor near the footlights during the initial "songs," teenagers reached across the footlights apparently trying to help themselves to pieces of his pants.

A tug-o'-war, which at first seemed jocular, then began between the teenagers on one side and members of Little Richard's band on the other for possession of the perspiring "body." Two girls scrambled on to the stage from the audience, evidently to help get the "singer" over the footlights, and before stadium attendants could get through the mob. Little Richard was lying on the floor in front of the stage being trampled. Little Richard was helped back to the stage, disappeared momentarily into the wings and returned to continue his act."[79]

Then in Sydney came the third and final sign.

That October in Australia, it was spring. Young screaming teenagers had filled a soccer stadium and turned it upside down. The culprits responsible for the shenanigans were American rock and roll singers, and at a time when President Eisenhower was sending troops into Little Rock, Arkansas schools to enforce racial integration in the States, the rock and rollers, all white southerners, were led by a black man—Little Richard—who two years earlier had launched rock & roll with rocket-age fury that upset the world.

Little Richard, drenched in sweat, "made an impressive entry," according to *The Age*, another Australian newspaper who wrote," [Little Richard] wearing a brilliant red coat over a canary yellow suit, topped off with a bright green turban, discarded all the trimmings until he was left with only pajama pants and the turban."[80]

Pounding on the piano and then dancing on top of it, he threw his bedazzled clothes into the crowd while he sang, *Keep A'Knockin'*, to the packed stadium. The Upsetters, his backing band, were fantastic, horns blowing, guitars strumming, booties shaking. Shrieking teenagers were causing a near riot trying to catch Richard's discarded clothes. Between his Sonic barrage with his band The Upsetters and his strip teasing energy, Richard aroused a feeding frenzy of teens fighting for his clothing. A newspaper reporter wrote that no one had ever seen or heard such violent movement an noise.

As the rock Raja got down to his turban and long underpants he looked up into the Australian night sky and saw something else that had never been seen before. A point of fire blaze across the violet sky winking with the menace of an evil eye.

It was a BRIGHT YELLOW FLAME!

Whatever it is, it was powerful enough to stop Little Richard from singing. He stood there looking at it and started quoting Revelations from the bible to the crowd:

*"A great sign was seen in heaven: a woman clothed
with the sun, and the moon under her feet."*

It looked as though the big ball of fire came directly
over the stadium about two or three hundred feet
above our heads," he later told his biographer, Charles
White. "It shook my mind." Little Richard suddenly
shocked the audience by getting off the piano and announcing to his adoring fans that in the middle of his
tour he would leave rock and roll to pursue Christian
ministry. "I got up from the piano and said, 'This is it.
I am through. I am leaving showbusiness to go back to
God.'"[81]

Richard walked off the stage and the audience boo'd
him. Backstage, Bumps Blackwell was in shock. He asked
if Richard had lost his mind. "You can't just ditch the tour
and leave a half million dollars' worth of canceled bookings. We'll be sued."

But Little Richard indeed did just that—left the tour
and a half million dollars' worth of canceled bookings.
Multiple lawsuits were to come. Richard scheduled the
band, crew and entourage on a flight back to the States
ten days earlier than originally planned. Later, he
learned that the flight he was originally booked on, Pan
Am Flight 7, crashed into the Pacific Ocean with all 44
passengers and crew members killed. "It was a sign," said
Richard—and Little Richard was always attuned to
signs.

What Richard actually saw in Australia that night was Sputnik, the Russian satellite, traveling 18,000 miles an hour in the sky. The singer mistook the satellite for a ball of fire—and a message from God. For Richard, a miracle was afoot. The bisexual black man who grew up poor in the Jim Crow South in Macon, Georgia, singing a wild, sexy, nonsense song that changed music forever, took it that God wanted him to stop. The message was clear: Little Richard had to leave show business, quit singing the devil's music, and get right with Lord.

When he got back to Los Angeles, he told Angel he couldn't see her anymore because he belonged to God now. Angel says that she left Richard in 1957 - the first of a number of temporary separations - even though the singer wanted to marry her.

That was it. It was 1955 to 1957, and just like that—for Little Richard, one of the greatest entertainers in Rock & Roll—singing the "Devil's" music...
...was over.

Side "B"

...and Religion

"Richard is a supreme star. A once in-a-millennium talent. And like many unique talents, he gets paranoid."

Robert "Bumps" Blackwell

Seven

Great GOD A'Mighty

"...There is no music like that music, no drama like the drama of the saints rejoicing, the sinners moaning, the tambourines racing, and all those voices coming together and crying holy unto the Lord.... I have never seen anything to equal the fire and excitement that sometimes, without warning, fill a church.... Nothing that has happened to me since equals the power and the glory that I sometimes felt... when the church and I were one."

—James Baldwin
The Fire Next Time

The Architect of Rock & Roll quit rock & roll altogether. He enrolled at Oakwood College in Huntsville, Alabama, a divinity school where he began studies to become a Seventh Day Adventist preacher.

The world was up in arms about his decision to leave secular music and the stories of *why* were more creative than a Harry Potter novel. A Chicago radio station reported that Little Richard had committed suicide. A newspaper announced that Richard was in a lunatic asylum. Others said that he had seen a vision and was in a monastery.

Arenas had been booked and deposits paid for nearly fifty engagements, but Richard refused to work—except for one friend—Alan Freed. To Richard, Freed was one of the greatest and could not be denied.

Freed had been a fair man to deal with. He always paid, unlike many of the promoters Richard had worked for—and Freed could have cared less about the White Citizens Council decrying: *"The screaming idiotic words and savage music of these records are undermining the morals of our white youth in America."*

So Richard would play his farewell concert for Freed at the Apollo Theater in New York to a hysterical crowd.

But that was it.

Praying that the worst had not indeed occurred, Art Rupe ordered a shutdown on any news out of Specialty Records, and all media inquiries were avoided. Rupe was in despair. He gave one interview to Billboard Music Week magazine saying, "Little Richard was so popular they could have recorded him blowing his nose and made a hit."[82]

Meanwhile Bumps Blackwell, Rupe's former A&R man, and now Little Richard's former manager left Specialty Records and took Sam Cooke with him. Rupe chose to turn his attention to Larry Williams— someone he had in the wings waiting to be turned loose.

Sensing he was being cheated Richard hired a lawyer to collect back royalties from Specialty Records that he estimated were at $25,000. The man who had given up his career to become Reverend Richard Penniman, filed a lawsuit for what he felt was due him.

> I never got what Elvis Presley got paid. I never got what Mick Jagger got paid," Richard lamented. "My friends and fans all over the world couldn't understand a guy at the height of his career quitting with the whole world in his hands. One reason was Art Rupe. It seemed that he wanted to buy me body and soul—with my own money. Bought things for me, then took it out of my money and said he had bought it. Can you imagine that?[83]

Richard lost that case, but agreed to cut one more session for Specialty Records. These would be his last recordings in the 1950s.

The Architect of Rock & Roll had found pleasure in his biblical studies, He became attracted to the idea of praising God through music and was singing in church again. He even recorded a gospel song with a gospel choir. He had found peace with God. His hair was a normal close crop and he was wearing corny regular suits and wing-tip shoes. The capes, glitter and make-up were gone, and he was preaching the Gospel to a whole new evangelical audience. "The kind of music I was singin' was demonic. God didn't want me doin' that."

This went on for a couple of years. At the Wildhorse Saloon in Nashville, Richard told the crowd: *"I just want y'all to know that Jesus is coming soon. He's been talking to me and wanted me to tell you that something's fixin' to happen to this world. Get close to God. All of you. Everybody, get closer."*

Reemerging as a Gospel singer after the refutation of his life with secular music was the perfect opportunity to remain true to his inner religious sense while still performing as an artist, and over the next four years, Reverend Penniman recorded for labels like End, Mercury, and Atlantic.

But although these labels had substantial followings, Gospel would not be as satisfying to Richard's ego since compared to rock and/or R&B, Gospel music comprised no more than a fraction of the rock & roll industry in terms of national sales or ratings on the major charts. So, unless your fame was well above the competition, becoming a star in the Gospel world, even with its financial rewards, would never be on the scale Little Richard had already attained in rock music.

Nevertheless, Richard was comfortable in the genre that had occupied him in childhood, and released an album entitled *God Is Real*. It achieved minor success in gospel terms.

Then Richard and a man named Joe Lutcher together formed what they called the *"Little Richard Evangelistic Team."* Richard started preaching, helping to feed people on skid row, ushering at tent meetings and taking Bible courses with the intention of becoming an ordained minister and to tour on the Gospel circuit the next year. All this scarcely 12 months following the fateful Australian tour.

While on his three-year course aimed at becoming ordained as an elder of the church, Richard indeed went on a Southern preaching and Gospel tour.

But in Atlanta, his demons began to spike.

Richard sought out Lee Angel who he discovered was working as a stripper at the 81 Theater. He went to see her. Angel had not desired to get mixed up with the church once Richard quit the business. When she saw Richard at the theater he had changed to her both in his appearance and himself. Though Richard wanted to go on seeing her, she couldn't bring herself to be with him. He was a preacher, she was a stripper—and never the twain shall meet again. It would be years before Richard saw Angel again.

As it turned out, the elders of the church were prevailing upon Richard to get married. Everybody told him he needed a wife—especially if he was serious about studying religion and becoming a minister. So Richard started taking those early steps toward finding a woman for the purpose of matrimony. That same year, 1957, while speaking at an evangelical convention, church elders introduced Richard to Ernestine Campbell, a pretty black secretary from Washington, D.C. Ernestine, a sweet, sensible girl just out of high school, was one of four daughters of a Washington navy family. She was working temporarily for the Department of the Navy before going to college when Richard entered her life. Richard and Ernestine dated for almost two years.

Meanwhile, from his arsenal of material that Richard recorded while still under contract to Specialty Records, Art Rupe had enough music to keep releasing Little Richard singles and albums for another year...

...Which is exactly what he did.

Rupe released *Good Golly Miss Molly Good,* which came out after *Long Tall Sally*. It was another song composed from one of the ditties Richard had partially made up while washing dishes in the Greyhound station in 1954. The song came out in February 1958 and subsequently went to #6 on the R&B charts and #10 on the Pop charts. It would be Little Richard's last top ten record and million seller.

Then while Richard and Ernestine were still dating,

Rupe released yet another Little Richard song, *Ooh My Soul*. The song was released in May 1958 made it to #15 on the R&B charts and #31 on the Pop charts.

Obviously having two hit songs in the marketplace and on the radio that year placed Richard in a precarious position since he had renounced secular music and re-signed himself to the church. Ever mindful of what he had to do to be true to the elders of the church and to God himself, he asked Ernestine to marry him.

The wedding took place at Richard's L.A. house at 1710 Virginia Road. It was scheduled for 9P.M. on July 11, 1959, but typically Richard was off somewhere and kept the bride, preacher, family, and guests waiting for six hours. Hardly the start of a dream marriage where real love was involved. It is difficult to tell whether he married Ernestine for traditional reasons or to promote the image of a newly rescued backslider, but Ernestine spoke on the matter:

> I met Richard in November 1957 when he came to speak at an evangelistic meeting being held by our church at a convention center in Washington, D.C., called Turner's Arena. I had heard of him, but I hadn't bought his records then because I wasn't into that kind of music. I was so impressed with him at the meeting. He was so clean-cut. He was suited and he looked just great. I had heard his music, of course, and heard interviews on the radio, but I had never seen him before. I don't know whether I fell in love with

him then." "[It] was a pretty long courtship, from November 1957 to July 1959. We had a happy marriage for a time, but I think from the beginning we didn't have a chance because I could not adjust to the lifestyle.[84]

Even Richard's brother, Charles, agreed the marriage was doomed. It would have been hard to find two people of more widely differing backgrounds and personalities than the ex-King of Rock & Roll and the shy, well-educated young secretary from Washington, D. C., and Charles felt the Church of God was attempting to manipulate Richard to do what they wanted him to do. It would be a union dominated by the needs of the church. "I felt they were using Ernestine to promote their own denomination," said Charles, "using Richard to bring other entertainers and other people to their church."[85]

Eight

Slippin' an' A'Slidin'

Earlier in 1959, Richard signed with a Los Angeles agency for an upcoming Gospel tour and in June of that year signed a contract with Gone Records. As the recording market for rock was so much more expansive than that of Gospel, the same was true of the audiences to be found for live performance touring. Rock tours maintained their audience appeal well past the borders of the United States.

But the number of Gospel disciples plummeted severely, not only by leaving the confines of the American Deep South, but even more severely by crossing into other countries. Add to that, Gospel was no longer an issue of mere taste. As time progressed in the rock revolution of "baby boomers," a newly empowered youth began to reject Gospel outright as a genre hostile to its brand of music.

For many, it represented an ideology of their parents, and in the midst of passing from adolescence to adulthood, such a thing was culturally unacceptable.

The decade of the 1950s was ending, and the number of devotees Little Richard lost—his former fans who became disenchanted with his transformation after having once been fully aware of his worldly nature—is unknown. There were many former fans who saw his conversion as hypocrisy and a betrayal of a music genre on its own path to becoming a religion with Little Richard as its Pope. That consideration may not have been on Richard's mind at the time, but his own war between the sacred and the secular was boiling over.

Richard remained productive and released three Gospel songs in 1960 including *Joy, Joy, Joy, He Got What He Wanted, He's Not Just a Soldier,* and *Crying in the Chapel.* Richard and Joe Lutcher set up a music publishing company together called Woodman Music Inc., just for religious music, and Richard also worked with Quincy Jones, an arrangement set up by Bumps Blackwell. People were so surprised by Richard's voice when it came to sacred music. Quincy called it a "Spirit feel" something that felt more like preaching rather than just singing. It was very moving. Said Quincy: "It was an experience that proved once again that deep religious feeling and fervor go hand in hand."[86]

After the Quincy Jones produced album *Little Richard King of the Gospel Singers* was released, Richard was inundated with offers to perform on the gospel circuit. He was finally doing what he wanted to do—the kind of music with a gospel feel and truth to it.

However, none of the releases rose beyond modest successes and Richard's prayed-for Gospel career never achieved lift-off—and certainly not financially.

Rock devotees fell away becoming disenchanted with their former hero now at work in the Gospel market. Additionally, established Gospel groups and their loyal audiences were highly suspicious of any Gospel singer who had led a secular existence before entering their genre. They were even more distrustful if that artist's life continued in its wanton ways during the years of recording in the Lord's name.

Where Richard's overt effeminacy may have been a valued and acceptable asset and part of the fabric in the rock world, it was certainly a drawback in the serious world of religious music. Especially in the Deep South.

"Little Richard" may have celebrated the audacious parts of his personality, but "Reverend Penniman" was obligated to hide it and transform this "down-low" behavior into a sexless charisma tailored to Biblical parables.

Fortunately for Richard, the vast, conservative audience of Southern religious culture believed that homosexuality was a defect into which one fell but not a condition inherited at birth. That being the pitch, Richard was able to renounce it as the sinful behavior of his past, not as a present danger in his core nature. This almost certainly helped gain access to theological study in Alabama, and disapproving audiences could forgive him—

perhaps even hail his conversion as a triumph over "the devil's " behavior. Thus, Richard tried to ignore and push his sexual nature as far down as possible, alternating between periods of renouncement and self-celebration. He affirmed the conservative viewpoint of the Southern church preaching that "homosexuality is contagious and not something you're born with." He and Ernestine then adopted a son, Danny, from a deceased church member's family.

But try as he may, the old demons were still doing battle as fiercely as ever within him. Tutors at Oakwood found Richard as frustrating a pupil as the teachers had at Richard's old high school in Macon.

He started turning up late for class, usually in one of his gaudily colored Cadillacs. He skipped lectures, and he was a disrupting influence in what was a quiet, well-ordered quasi-religious liberal arts college. He began to entertain the students with echoes of his illustrious past. The students loved it.

The deans didn't.

He even held up a recording session that Bumps Blackwell kindly set up for him, where he was supposed to be laying tracks for a gospel album. "We were recording one session on Sunday, and there were forty musicians in the studio on double time," said Blackwell: "Richard was due to arrive at 10 A.M. and he kept us all waiting around until 8 P.M. Then he turned up and announced calmly, "The Lord does not want me to record today." Manny Klein, who had organized the session, broke down and wept."[87] Said Richard:

> They had discovered that I was a homosexual and I re-sented the discovery. I had worked with a young guy and I had him show himself to me. I didn't touch him, but he went back and told his father, who was a deacon of the church. The church had a board meeting to let me know that it was wrong. I was so mad.[88]

One can only assume what the conversation was like when Richard was reprimanded. Something like this?— "The Devil is powerful. Maybe more powerful than God." "Richard, remember, once Adam and Eve ate from the Tree of Knowledge, they realized they were naked in the garden. The Lord gave them freedom of choice. The inclination for sex became a part of them. They didn't need an external tempter like the serpent to incite them. That tempter was now in their psyches—especially sexual passion which can be stronger than the desire to praise God." And then Richard attempting a cry for help, "Yes, but can't you help me?"

These are the kinds of arguments regarding his contradictory Old Testament morality versus his flagrant avant-gardness that Richard would have with himself all his life. Whether Richard asked the young male student to expose himself or if Richard exposed his own self to the student, his church, being who they were with their abject far right ideologies, politely asked Richard to leave.

They say the Bible is a hypocrite's favorite prop, but it was no more a "gimmick"—as Ernestine Campbell Penniman called Richard's cross-dressing stage act—than the performer's actual sexual preference.

Soon Richard, without his church anchor, yet praying for the redemption many gay men in that era felt was necessary to hold Hell at bay, but losing the battle, fell back into his old ways. He began his voyeurism again—going to public men's rooms and watching men urinate. He'd be there sometimes for over an hour.

In early 1962, Little Richard was arrested again after he was caught spying on men in a men's toilet at a Trailways bus station in Long Beach, California. Per Richard:

> I had dropped a guy off at the Trailways bus station in Long Beach. I went down into the restroom, to look, to see who was doing what, to watch people take out and urinate, like I always did. While I was down there the police raided the place. Once you walk into a raid you don't get out of it. These young boys with jeans on came into the place and pulled out their badges and said, "You're under arrest." Just boys! And while I was trying to talk to them, 'cos they wouldn't let me go, they hit me and knocked blood out of my face. My face was bleeding. I didn't know what was going on. I wasn't innocent. I went there and I got caught and I had to pay the price. My lawyer told me to plead guilty and let it go. He said don't say

anything, 'cos they'll make a case out of nothing. So I paid the fine.[89]

But this fine was emotionally larger. Richard's slow reversion to his former lifestyle, coming on top of two and a half years of neglect and turmoil, proved the last straw for Ernestine. She could not take it, thus becoming another casualty of Richard's indecision regarding his sexually fluid, swinging lifestyle, faith, or desire to sing secular.

In a move that, at least to the outside world, appeared to be Richard hurling his robes of monastic life away, he divorced Ernestine Campbell, or rather Ernestine divorced him. Even if she didn't (or chose not to) see him as gay, she filed for divorce after two and a half years of marriage. It's one thing to stand by your man while he's doing the Lord's work, but quite another when he's batting for the other team at the same time. She cited "extreme cruelty by the infliction of grievous mental suffering."

The action was uncontested.

Ernestine was right. I was a neglectful husband. A terrible husband..." said Richard. "...We were not compatible the way we should have been. When I met Ernestine I liked her a whole lot, but I never loved her in the way a man should love his wife. I loved her more like a sister. Ernestine was jealous and she had reason enough to be, because I wasn't a husband. I didn't give her any attention. I was gay and I wasn't concerned. I was like a lot of men today who have got wives. I had to think of someone else to be with her, to be complete. I was thinking about Johnny. About Jimmy. I had to think about someone I wanted and couldn't get.[90]

Apparently, until then, Ernestine had been oblivious.

If he was gay he was very good about hiding it from me! And if he was he never wanted it to affect me. I don't recollect any incident that indicated that," said Ernestine. "It was only things that people said. There were times when I felt that I wanted to ask him about it because people, being unkind, or perhaps not realizing they were being unkind, asked me about it. Why he dressed like that. Why he acted like that. But it never affected my relationship with him because it had nothing to do with me. I accepted his act.[91]

Okay. But what appears more obvious, is that Ernestine wanted another kind of marriage for herself, another kind of man. Perhaps what she wanted was one who came home for dinner each night, who didn't have throngs of screaming fans at stage doors, one who knew whether he loved God, or raunchy music.

Or most likely—one who was clear if he wanted a woman, a man —or both. Richard admitted that he loved both performing and the road. To not do so would be for him not to be true to himself.

The divorce would be final in 1963.

Meanwhile, after a total of five years of little success as a gospel performer Richard found himself being pulled by the power of the secular back into the lure of Rock & Roll. Like a contemporary Franz Liszt who scheduled lavish, sexy concerts one year and retreat to an abbey the next, Little Richard and Reverend Richard continued their "one-foot-in, one-foot-out" dance of "Is he Rock, or is he religion" into the early '60s when rock & roll music and the rewards it offered were beginning to re-capture his fascination again.

Bumps and Richard had dinner together in Los Angeles on a warm spring California day. Bumps asked Richard if he was satisfied with his new religious life because it sure looked like the same old one. He told Richard he could be making "some long cash with your old act." For Blackwell, it felt as though Richard and God were at odds.

Bumps suggested that a "gospel tour" in Europe could be put together for Richard with Don Arden, a promoter he knew in London. "Folks just want 'Little Richard.'"

At this deeply traumatic point in Richard's life, Blackwell sought out Don Arden who was assembling a tour. Arden, father of Sharon, who would become the future Mrs. Ozzy Osbourne, had already promoted successful tours in Europe for Jerry Lee Lewis and Brenda Lee.

Despite Richard's retirement his records were still selling well in England, even though Rock & Roll was in a downward slump in the United States.

With Don Arden, the persona that was Little Richard could resurface, and perhaps there was a way in which he could resurrect his former glory—even though Richard would only accept Arden's offer to tour Europe in a package show if he did his "new" act. Not knowing that Richard's "new" act was mostly sacred music, an excited Arden sent over a contract with Little Richard as the main attraction to close the show each night.

It was 1962—and Richard's first comeback was on!

Little Richard with The Upsetters

Nine

Britain, Billy and the Beatles

Before Little Richard left for Europe, he had heard about a young black musical prodigy who was playing keyboard for Mahalia Jackson. When Richard heard the young man, he was flabbergasted and had to have him on his tour.

William Everett Preston, known as "Billy" Preston, was then sixteen years old and entirely self-taught. He'd never had a music lesson. By the age of ten, he was playing organ onstage backing several gospel singers like Jackson who was Richard's all-time favorite gospel singer. Richard instantly hired Preston to play organ and Preston was excited to be part of Little Richard's European tour.

Richard easily identified with Billy's music because it was saturated in gospel traditions which Richard loved and they both understood the trip to be a gospel tour of Europe. Richard, then 30 years old, immediately took Billy under his wing and gave him a musical platform.

Billy Preston, 1972

What Richard did not know at the time was he and Billy had far more in common.

Billy was also struggling with his sexuality and its affects and consequences on his religious life. Both men were brought up in the African-American gospel tradition. Billy Preston was a committed Christian throughout his life and openly expressed his faith in such later works as his 1970s hit *That's the Way God Planned It* and *With You I'm Born Again*.

However, his personal beliefs were sometimes at odds with the attitudes and musical expressions of the secular world of rock & roll in which he often worked, and his burgeoning same-sex feelings. He became close to Little Richard, and one cannot help but wonder if at some point on the tour they had a tentative conversation about it, since their struggles were so analogous. Said Keith Richards in his famous 2011 autobiography, *Life*:

> [H]e [Billy Preston] was gay at a time when nobody could be openly gay, which added difficulties to his life...[92]

Preston looked up to Little Richard like a big brother, and this would be his first tour of Europe. He was excited. So was Richard. Since Richard refused to fly anymore since the incident with the 1957 plane crash in Australia, he, Preston, and Richard's back-up band the Upsetters set sail from New York to England on an aging ocean liner called the S.S. Rotterdam. Onboard, Richard and Billy had lots of time to bond during the weeklong.

Richard arrived in Britain at a time when England worshipped all things Americana—and black Americana at that—from across a seemingly unbridgeable cultural abyss. The British had assiduously studied and reproduced Blues and soul music (to the best of their abilities) in an attempt to attain some degree of empathy with their transcendent outpourings of joy and pain. They were trying to crack the facade of true British reserve by appropriating the persona of the black Blues singing soul man.

When Richard got there he found a London that knew more about Motown, Mingus, Diddley and Muddy Waters than all but a few white Americans.

However, the cultural context from which the music had derived was still a mystery to them. Yes, they understood the vocal tricks and guitar licks, and many of them could reproduce them—as Richard would discover with Paul McCartney of the Beatles later, but actual contact with black Americans had left them with big question marks on their faces.

Little Richard on the other hand understood white bohemia quite instinctively and white English Rock &

Roll bohemia in particular after all he shared many of its tastes and obsessions and was perfectly happy to give them exactly what they wanted.

Richard was flamboyant, exhibitionistic and fond of being photographed surrounded by admiring white fans. He was almost totally lacking in the kind of dignity, discipline and restraint which black America had come to demand from its entertainers then.

To say that Richard had no black constituency at all, though, is to pander to racist myth. Vernon Reid, a black, British-born American guitarist and songwriter and the founder and primary songwriter of the rock band *Living Colour,* explained it to writer Charles Shaar Murray.

> You have to look at the society which makes us view ourselves a certain way. On one level the idea of being flashy or outspoken is appealing because from the time that you're small if you're a black person there is a social move to negate your existence what is it like to be nothing they don't come out and say you're nothing. But a band aid is flesh colored even if it's not the color of your flesh. It's a lot better now but at the time Richard was coming along that was the status quo so when you see people who are black being outrageous they are asserting themselves. There is a psychological need to assert themselves because there's a feeling that if you're black you're not anything.[93]

Richard's first European performance was set for the Gaumont Theater in Doncaster, England. Doncaster was the perfect place to start the tour. It is a large town in South Yorkshire, England located about 177 miles north of London, and until 1974 included the West Riding of York. Any of you who watched *Downton Abbey* know that story took place in Yorkshire and a train was necessary to reach London.

The bill in Doncaster was to include Sam Cooke. Cooke, who had made a name for himself with such hits as *Chain Gang, You Send Me, Cupid,* and others, started out like Little Richard singing religious music with the Soul Stirrers. Art Rupe, head of Specialty Records, the label of the Soul Stirrers, gave his blessing for Cooke to start recording secular music. But he became unhappy about the type of music Cooke and producer **Bumps Blackwell** were making. Rupe expected Cooke's secular music to be similar to that of another Specialty Records artist—Little Richard. When Rupe walked in on a recording session and heard Cooke covering Gershwin, he was furious. After an argument between Rupe and Blackwell, Cooke and Blackwell left the label.[94]

Because of heavy fog in England, Cooke and his manager J.W. Alexander missed a connection flight and were painfully late. They missed the first show.

Meanwhile, Little Richard and Billy Preston had come to England under the impression they were doing a gospel tour and for that first show Richard came out in a religious robe and his hair tame. He started singing

Peace in the Valley and *I Believe*—his sacred music. His fans were flummoxed. They were clamoring for what they wanted—his known music—and they became confused and bewildered. They didn't know Richard as a gospel singer and wanted the "Real" Little Richard.

As he sang, Richard could tell he was losing the audience. There was no energy from them—something he fed off of—and there were groans and an air of palpable discontent—with none more disgruntled than promoter

Don Arden backstage sweating in a panic. If this was to be Little Richard's intended set, and Richard was the star attraction, the word-of-mouth would kill the shows. Arden stood to lose hundreds of thousands of investor dollars. The tour could flop or even be cancelled. Twenty-five cities had been lined up

Sam Cooke, circa 1960

for the next two months. This was a disaster in the making.

When Sam Cooke and his manager finally arrived at the theater for the second show of the day, Arden was at wits end. He asked J.W. Alexander to please help him out. "Speak to Richard. Tell him he's got to go back to the old stuff. That's what the kids want to hear."

But Alexander just grinned. He told Arden that if he knew Little Richard correctly—a man with whom he had worked in the old Specialty Records days—that Richard was highly competitive. He told Arden that if Richard took one look at Sam Cooke's fabulous act coupled with Cooke's masculine good looks and ability to move women to lose their minds, he'll come around—on his own. "Trust me, Sam'll just go out there and he'll kill that audience. Then Richard will come out and take care of himself."

It was a brilliant ploy. After that tepid audience response to his gospel music, Richard realized during shows that he had to do something to keep his audience.

At the second show of the night, Sam Cooke went on. Sure enough, J.W. Alexander was right. Sam Cooke tore it up. He laid the fans in the aisles turning in a powerhouse performance with *Twistin' The Night Away*. The applause lasted well into the intermission.

Richard was watching all of this from the wings simmering. While the other second-half opening acts were did their thing, he talked with the band and prepared a new presentation. He was not having it.

Sam Cooke would not win the night. Oh no. Nobody upstages Little Richard.

Finally, Little Richard's name was announced. *"The Innovator, The Emancipator, The One. The Only. Architect of Rock & Roll...Little Richard!"*

The audience then heard the wailing chords of Billy Preston's organ in the dark. Richard spent a minute in absolute blackness warming up with Preston, creating an unbearable tension with the audience. Suddenly, a solo spotlight finds Richard with a foot-high pompadour wig, standing at a grand piano in the center of the stage wearing all-white.

He starts pounding out *Long Tall Sally.*

> Well long, tall Sally she's
> Built for speed, she got
> Everything that Uncle John need,
> Oh baby, yeah baby, woo baby
> Havin' me some fun tonight, yeah[95]

The audacity of it all shatters the house and they erupt into CHEERS! In seeing Sam Cooke's reception, Richard's ego was in high drive and he was back rockin' and rollin', which Arden had hoped for. With high-jumping, hip-shaking, spine-tingling renditions of his perennial hits, *Lucille, Good Golly Miss Molly, and Tutti Frutti,* which were performed with awesome energy and dynamism, Little Richard kept the entire audience spellbound, on their feet, and in near-hysteria. Then he walked off to a thunderous ovation.

If anything was going through Richard's mind when exited the stage, it had to be "Take that, Sam Cooke."

It was a night to remember—the night a king returned to his throne—and it was repeated everywhere he appeared all over Europe.

Billy Preston was surprised when the tour changed from what he thought was a gospel tour to a rock & Roll tour. But it excited him. He had never played that kind of music and loved the audience response—especially when they would gather outside the stage door and call out his name and ask for autographs. Thereafter, Billy Preston showed what he could do on the organ to enhance Little Richard's performances.

In the seaside resort of Brighton, the Hippodrome crowd also erupted and there was hysteria the likes of which had never been seen in an English venue. Little Richard whipped the audience into such a frenzy that hall management warned that the show would be stopped. Ignoring them, Richard jumped on and off the piano, threw his jacket, tie, and shirt to the audience, leaped into the orchestra pit—causing a rush of girls to the front of the auditorium to try to touch him, and finished his act on his knees soaked with sweat and wrapped in a bathrobe.

Richard wrecked the place. The kids got so wild that when Richard and the band came out to get into the bus hordes of fans all gathered around shaking the bus screaming. It took an hour before crowd control could clear them and the group could get away.

The self-proclaimed "king *and queen* of Rock & Roll" was back in business with his former band, The Upsetters, and a number of record companies took notice. They invited him back to the studio, but they were mostly only interested in repackaging his old hits. Specialty, in five sessions attempted to rekindle the 1957 magic. Richard had to show them—to show Europe—that he still had it whether in gospel or Rock & Roll.

Ten

He's Baaack!!

At Mansfield's Granada Theatre, Richard polished his act and introduced some new ideas. A huge grand piano stood in the middle of the stage, but no Richard. The tension mounted as all the theater lights went out, leaving only a spotlight on the piano. The music stopped. The audience held its breath.

Then, from the back of the auditorium came Richard's incredible and unmistakable voice shouting out the titles of his hits: *Long Tall Sally Tutti Frutti,* and *Good Golly Miss Molly.* He ran down the aisle toward the stage, dressed in a white silk suit, not quite avoiding the clutching hands of a delirious crowd. One of them ripped off his white bow tie. A giant leap took him onto the edge of the orchestra pit and from there onto the stage where he grabbed the microphone and began singing *Good Golly Miss Molly* and pounding the piano.

The next stop on the tour was at the Tower theater in New Brighton which was twenty minutes from Liverpool. There, Richard met and befriended a group of long-mop-haired white lads barely out of their teens who had become popular in the Merseyside area of the UK. They were his opening act and sounded as though they had steeped themselves in Little Richard tea.

Unknown at the time, in two years they would become John, Paul, George and Ringo of The Beatles. But then, all they did was watch Richard perform from backstage too frightened to approach him.

At the first performance, the press was out in full force. Richard had told *Record Mirror*, "I sing gospel songs but with a beat. God has told me to do this." But Richard was rock 'n' rolling. Cameras flashed, reporters jockeyed for position and interviews. Everyone was standing on their seats. Halfway through a mind-blowing version of *Lucille,* Richard leaped onto the piano top, mike in hand, and boogied around.

Then, without warning, he fell rigid from the piano as if hit by a high-powered shotgun. The band stuttered to a halt, and the good-time atmosphere ended. Richard lay like a corpse in the center of the stage, as Bob Bain, the stage manager, rushed frantically onstage and asked:

"Is there a doctor in the house?"

A member of Sounds Incorporated ran offstage shouting for help. The audience was frozen into silence. All one

could see was a tidal wave of shocked, strained, and anx-
ious faces as a verbal buzz of concern rose.

Suddenly from centerstage, Little Richard's voice
burst forth, very much alive singing, *"Awop Bop Aloo
Mop Awop Bam Boom... Tutti Frutti..."*

Inebriated with joy, the audience surged forward and
the hysteria caused the stage staff to bring down the
safety curtain, ending the show.

Richard's amazing performance and presence attracted a tremendous amount of press commentary. The
Beatles' manager,
Brian Epstein, had
the idea of using the
publicity generated
by Richard to help
promote his protégés
who were having a lo-
cal hit in Liverpool
with their single,
Love Me Do backed
with *Please Please
Me.* Epstein ap-
proached Richard to
do two extra dates

there at the end of his tour, one at the Tower, New
Brighton, and the other at the Empire Theatre.

The Beatles were the main support group and several
other Merseyside bands filled in the rest of the bill.

Thereafter was a series of one-nighters which, for any other human being, would have been taxing and exhausting. Not for Little Richard. He danced, sang, shimmied, screeched and "wooo'd" his way through the rest of the 19 different British cities electrifying audiences and reminding them why he and he alone was the one true King of Rock & Roll.

This is just a sample of his tour schedule just in England in 1962: Gaumont Theatre, Doncaster-Oct 8, 1962; Granada Cinema, Mansfield-Oct 9, 1962; Birmingham Town Hall, Birmingham-Oct 10, 1962; Granada Cinema, Grantham-Oct 11, 1962; Tower Ballroom, New Brighton, Little Richard, The Beatles Oct 12, 1962; Granada Cinema, Woolwich-Oct 13, 1962; Hippodrome, Brighton-Oct 14, 1962; Colston Hall, Bristol-Oct 15, 1962; Gaumont Theatre, Southampton-Oct 16, 1962; Granada Cinema, Bedford-Oct 17, 1962; Granada Cinema, Maidstone-Oct 18, 1962; Granada Theatre, Kingston-upon-Thames-Oct 19, 1962; Adelphi Cinema, Slough-Oct 20, 1962; The Granada Cinema, Walthamstow, London Oct 21, 1962; Newcastle City Hall, Newcastle - Oct 22, 1962; Sheffield City Hall, Sheffield - Oct 23, 1962; Granada Theatre, Kettering - Oct 24, 1962; Granada Theatre, Harrow - Oct 25, 1962; Granada Cinema, Tooting, London - Oct 27, 1962; Little Richard, The Beatles; Empire Theatre, Liverpool – Oct 28, 1962.

Little Richard remembers:

Brian Epstein booked me to play at the Cavern with them. A couple of weeks later he had me headlining a big concert at a theater in Liverpool. They [The Beatles] were a support band, with the Swinging Blue Jeans, Cilla Black, and Gerry and the Pacemakers. The Beatles went on and sang 'Love Me Do.' They couldn't do my numbers, 'Lucille' and 'Long Tall Sally,' 'cos I was there. When they came off, Brian Epstein said to me, "Richard, I'll give you fifty percent of the Beatles." I couldn't accept 'cos I never thought they would make it. Brian Epstein said, 'Take the masters [of Beatles songs] back to America with you and give them to the record company for me.' I didn't do that, but I did call up some people for them. I phoned Art Rupe and I also got in touch with Vee Jay, but I didn't take a piece of them.[96]

Looking back on that decision now I'm sure Richard regrets his business choice, but back then he was coming from a pure place. He loved working with the Beatles and tried to help them. His favorites were Paul McCartney and George Harrison. He thought Paul and George were sweet with humble personalities. In his own words, they were more "submissive" types versus John and Ringo who were on occasion slightly aloof to him. Paul would come into Richard's dressing room, sit down, and just look at him. He would watch Richard's every move.

Many times the group had sandwiches or sodas with Richard, or when they didn't have money, Richard paid for their food. Other times they would harmonize, and Richard showed them performance tricks.

Richard's eclectic style turned out to be an outstanding influence on the Beatles sound, especially on Paul McCartney who loved Little Richard:

> Man, we'd met our idol who we stole everything from. I never thought I'd meet Little Richard. The first song I ever sang in public was *Long Tall Sally*. ...I celebrated my last day of term at the Liverpool Institute by taking in my guitar, climbing on a desk in the classroom and singing my two party pieces, *Long Tall Sally* and *Tutti Frutti*.[97]

Paul would say, *"Oh, Richard! You're my idol. Just let me touch you."* He wanted to learn Richard's "woooo's" and asked Richard to teach it to him. So Richard accommodated. He'd sit at the piano yodeling "Woooo!" and Paul would follow singing "Woooo!" until finally he got it right. *"In our imaginations back then,"* said Paul, *"John was Buddy (Holly) and I was Little Richard... You're always someone else when you start."* The adulation was obvious. Just listen to McCartney's "wooo's" in *I Saw Her Standing There*. It came straight from Little Richard."[98]

Richard would invite them onstage to sing *Long Tall Sally* and Paul could not contain himself. Infatuated by Richard's vocal prowess, McCartney even tried to impersonate Richard's style during his performances. The Lad from Liverpool could imitate Richard's voice fairly well. *"I could do Little Richard's voice, which is a wild,*

*hoarse, screaming thing, it's like an out-of-body experi-
ence. You have to leave your current sensibilities and go
about a foot above your head to sing it."*[99] Not many
people could wail like Richard, but Paul got close with his
screaming lead vocals on The Beatles cover of *Good
Golly Miss Molly, Tutti-Frutti* and *Lucille*. His fondness
for falsetto vocals also came directly from Little Richard
and Paul later joked that Richard never let him forget it.

In addition to Paul, John Lennon was also a fan:

> Little Richard was one of the all-time greats. The first
> time I heard him, a friend of mine had been to Hol-
> land and brought back a 78 with Long Tall Sally on
> one side, and Slippin' and Slidin' on the other. It blew
> our heads—we'd never heard anybody sing like that
> in our lives and all those saxes playing like crazy.[100]

Once, while on the tour of clubs in Hamburg, Germany, Richard threw his shirt into the audience during a
performance. At a later date, Paul went out and got one
of his best shirts and said, "Take it, Richard. I'll feel bad
if you don't take it." Richard did and Paul exclaimed,
"Just think—Little Richard's got on my shirt. I can't believe it."

Richard threw the shirt into the audience at the next
performance. So much for the gift. But Richard and Paul
developed an especially close relationship while in Hamburg, and for the next two months the "Fab Four," the
"Beautiful" Architect and young Billy Preston became a
love fest. They hung out at clubs all over Germany.

There is a hilarious clip I recently found on YouTube from 2017 where Paul tells Ronnie Wood of The Rolling Stones (both elder statesmen now) on Ron's talk show *The Ronnie Wood Show* about his time with Richard on the road in Hamburg.

In addition to talking about how he used to sing *Long Tall Sally* as a teenager in school, Paul mused:

> Richard had one of those voices you couldn't believe.... It was one of the first wild, high voices... It was all from Gospel. Richard was a quite a character. I loved it when he would do that steaming thing—tie his hair in a scarf, then lean over a pot of steaming water with a towel over his head to help get his voice ready before a performance. I started doing that. I copied him. Then Richard would look up into the mirror after and say to himself, [does a high-pitched Little Richard impression] 'I'm so beautiful. I can't help it. I'm so beautiful.[101]

Paul then laughed. So did I. It sounded as though it was such a great time for all of them—and a learning experience for The Beatles.

The flamboyant Richard even became a huge fan of The Fab Four later saying: "I've never heard that sound from English musicians before. Honestly, if I hadn't seen them with my own eyes I'd have thought they were a colored group from back home."[102]

Richard also got along very well with Brian Epstein who later reunited Richard with James Brown in

Brussels. The two had been close friends since their teen years.

Clearly, Richard was on a roll. He was beloved to his fans in Europe and having a ball with his tour members. Not only did Little Richard leave the good Reverend Penniman behind in his return to the rock and roll world, but he went so far as to realign himself with Art Rupe and Specialty Records, indicating that the pre-Australian tour strife was not of a lethal enough nature to preclude the two from working together again. The reunion was urged on by The Beatles, who later recorded their own version of "Long Tall Sally" in 1964.

Said Preston, "I remember how excited the Beatles were to meet Richard. He had been their idol for years. In Hamburg they'd always be with him asking him questions about America, the cities, the stars, the movies, Elvis, and all that. And when Richard left to go back to the United States they cried."[103]

But so did Billy Preston. While on tour with Richard and The Beatles, he and the "Fab Four" also became very close. They loved Billy's organ playing—and Little Richard, who was very observant, saw this.

"Richard left me in Hamburg without a ticket home," lamented Billy.

It was true. Somehow, Preston was left stranded when the ticket for the train was not left for him. A controversy exists about what happened. Preston claimed that when the tour finished in Hamburg he was to meet Little Richard at the train station to get his ticket for the ship back to America. Richard never showed. So Preston went to Don Arden's office to see if it was left with him. It wasn't. Fortunately for Preston, The Beatles were in Arden's office at the time and felt sorry for him. They immediately offered him the opportunity to play with them.

But according to Little Richard, Preston wasn't left stranded. He wasn't ready to come back to the States. Richard says he left the ticket with Arden then had to leave to catch the ship for America when Preston wasn't where he said he would be. Richard does admit that he could see Preston was enjoying his time with The Beatles.

In any event, for young Billy Preston, this may have been the best thing to happen to him as he became so famous playing with The Beatles, he was soon dubbed: "the fifth Beatle."

He would go on to embark on his own as a successful solo artist recording for such labels as Apple Records, Motown, A&M Records, Derby, Vee-Jay Records, Capitol, and Buddah Records, and creating hits like *Will It Go Round in Circles, Nothing from Nothing, Get Back, and With You I'm Born Again* (with Syreeta). He remained a hit maker until a year before his death on June 6, 2006 from kidney disease at age 59.

It was a real loss for Richard.

Eleven

Sticks 'n' Stones
1963

Little Richard came home from his 1962 tour of Europe in December. He was invigorated and raring to go again in the States as a cherished and adored Rock & Roll star. He wanted to reemerge with some new songs as opposed to singing his older hits.

He was inspired by Sam Cooke's success and could see how much money Cooke was earning. Plus his business acumen led Cooke to open his own recording studio and take charge of his product. Richard wanted to mirror Cooke's success in the U.S. especially having had a taste of stardom and all its accoutrements again in Europe.

Though he felt guilty that he had left the Rock of Ages in America for the Rock & Roll of Europe, he still had his family in Los Angeles to take care of. Perhaps the robes of religion and sacred music could wait just a bit longer for its fullest expression. So Richard decided not to disclose to his family what happened in London and that he'd abandoned gospel for "Good Golly" for a little while.

However, finding success in his home country was proving arduous. He could not get bookings on television shows and was stymied by why he still wasn't asked to do the Ed Sullivan Show—which he should have done at least once in '57 or '58 when his first hits were huge. Now he was watching lesser known talents on the show.

It finally dawned on him after Bumps Blackwell had to explain with some difficulty that Richard had been off the scene for over five years with his move into the ministry and gospel music coupled with a tour of Europe. American audiences had simply moved on—many of them to singers Richard had inspired.

In the next year, Richard received his degree in Theology and was contemplating a full-time return to the ministry especially when he and his family were watching television on a hot August day and saw Dr. Martin Luther King give his iconic "I Have A Dream" speech on the steps of the Lincoln Memorial in Washington D.C. during the 1963 March on Washington for Jobs and Freedom. Seeing and hearing Dr. King seemed to motivate Richard who could envision himself holding millions of people rapt with his oratory in the same way he did with his music.

It was underscored when Richard saw, just behind Dr. King, his old friend and favorite gospel singer Mahalia Jackson—who had sung at the event and could audibly be heard urging Dr. King to, *"Tell 'em 'bout the dream,*

Martin. Tell 'em 'bout the dream," to which Dr. King moved away from his prepared speech and extemporaneously preached*: "I have a dream that one day on the red hills of Georgia the sons of former slaves and the sons of former slave owners will be able to sit down together at the table of brotherhood..."*

While Richard was watching Dr. King, finding himself moved as a black man who wanted change and growth as an artist, and feeling emboldened in his own dream to be a great orator applying at either a pulpit or in a stadium, Don Arden called him from London in a panic.

Arden begged Richard to help him out and join a package tour which had already begun—to possibly save it. It would be a 30-date tour scheduled to last 36 days, and had gotten under way on Sunday, 29 September 1963 at London's New Victoria Theatre.

"It was a last minute thing to get me on the tour," said Richard. "They had my old friend Bo Diddley and The Everly Brothers as headliners, but the bookings weren't going too well."

It was true. In the first week of the tour, it became clear to Arden that the Everlys, whose star had diminished since the emergence of The Beatles and other beat groups, were not selling enough tickets. Said Arden:

> "The Everly Brothers had definitely had it. I phoned up Little Richard and said, 'Richard you've gotta help me out' He said 'Ok'."[104]

Richard had not wanted to do another tour—especially when he still had a toe dipped into the religious market and desired a return to it. Another tour meant he was back doing the "Devil's music."

But a 'bird in the hand' was better and Richard gathered The Upsetters again, sans Billy Preston, and went back to London. Even though he hated flying and had sailed to the UK for his 1962 tour, Don Arden needed him immediately. So he had to fly, but with great reluctance.

Don Arden had considered an R&B first half with the Rolling Stones, Bo Diddley and Little Richard but he dropped this idea, preferring Richard to close the first half and Diddley to open the second.

Little Richard arrived in the UK the day before the Watford's Gaumont performance and was in for a surprise. During the year, the Beatles had taken the UK by storm and many other UK beat bands were on the charts. When he arrived at the airport, the only thing all the press wanted to know was what he thought of the Beatles. Richard was cordial and complimentary, but his age-old sense of competition rose within him again.

He gave an interview to *Record Mirror* speaking in the language of billboards by saying, "Little Richard Is Something To See, Something To Hear. It Will Be The Exciting Little Richard In His Amazing Role as An Atomic Bomb." He commented on the new beat trends and by the time the tour reached Watford's Gaumont cinema, its seventh date, Little Richard had already in-creased ticket sales.

He had also created a new look for his act. He would wear close-fitting shiny suits and unlike 1962, he would not feign a collapse on stage followed by a wild revival. No, he had something far more spectacular in mind. He knew The Beatles and other UK bands previously and he knew that something new was happening and he had to outshine everybody.

At Richard's first appearance he sang *Long Tall Sally, Rip It Up, Tutti Frutti* and *Lucille,* provoking the Everlys who had *Rip It Up and Lucille* in their own set list.

More to the point, it was not a 10 minute act. Richard went berserk, shedding his jacket, tie, shirt and shoes. He climbed onto the piano and sang with the audience. The effect was sensational. He stopped the show and en-cored with *Jenny Jenny* and *Hound Dog* while brilliantly supported by The Flintstones who were also on the bill. The closure of the first half was delayed by 20 minutes.

Writer JH reviewing the show for Disc magazine said:

Little Richard's dynamic debut on the Everly Brothers package tour at Watford on Saturday proved that he is still the greatest, wildest performer in the world. Every Little Richard hit from 'Lucille' to 'Good Golly Miss Molly' was hurled at the audience which stamped, raved and yelled with the artist. The old wild action was there and Little Richard's complete perfor-mance was charged with shouts of 'All right!' between songs. By the end of his act, he was stripped of all his clothing except for his blue mohair pants. After he closed the first half, the yells for an encore lasted almost five minutes. This man is tremendous.[105]

The Everly's manager, Jack Rael, complained to Don Arden that Little Richard was allowed too much time, but Arden sided with Richard. Arden had already asked Richard to stay on for the Shirelles tour which would feature Duane Eddy or Chuck Berry. He had been thinking of making an Everly Brothers special with ITV producer Johnnie Hamp for Granada Television. But now Little Richard seemed like a much better idea.

Although Don and Phil Everly loved Richard's music, they became increasingly irritated by the way his set ran over and how he acted as though he was the bill topper.

In addition to his friends Bo Diddley and the Everly's there was a little-known band touring with them as the opening act. They were the Rolling Stones. The Stones had a charismatic lead singer named Mick Jagger, who hopped and jumped all over the stage with a frenetic energy that almost matched Richard's. Don Arden knew that the Stones, a white, London R&B combo, were the most promising new kids on the block. Their first single, a cover of Chuck Berry's *Come On*, was released in June 1963 and reviewed by Don Nicholl in *Disc*. "The Beatles I'm told were among the first people to recommend the Rolling Stones to Decca." Said Arden, "Everybody was talking about the Rolling Stones and I was able to get them for the ridiculous fee of £40 a night."[106]

As with The Beatles, lead singer Mick Jagger of the Stones would stand backstage watching Richard's every move like it was assigned homework. Jagger studied Richard like a yogi at the feet of the Mahatma absorbing how Richard wiggled his hips, strutted onstage, or flaunted his flamboyance. Jagger even mouthed the lyrics to Richard's songs as if in a rehearsal. Said Jagger in Record Mirror magazine:

> I had never seen him before on the stage. I'd heard so much about the audience reaction that I thought there must be some exaggeration...but not so. There's no single phrase to describe his hold on the audience. To some it may excite. To others it may terrify. At times it reminds one of the Rock and Roll riots of early '57 and '58 with the whole theatre jumping as the audience, mainly boys, jumped up on stage and jived in the aisles.[107]

Bill Wyman, Mick Jagger, Charlie Watts, Brian Jones, Keith Richards. The Rolling Stones 1963

At one show, Little Richard had a long pounding introduction from Terry Slater of the Flintstones, who was his backing band, and everyone wondered where Little Richard was. Soon, he came screaming down the aisle singing *Lucille* and he followed it with *Long Tall Sally, Tutti Frutti, Whole Lotta Shakin' Goin' On, and Rip It Up*, but really he could have been singing anything. His showmanship was re-markable and at one point he clenched the top of a chair with his teeth, held it aloft and then did a wild dance around the front of the stage. He stripped to his underpants and put on a dressing-gown as he closed with 'Hound Dog'. He had been on stage for over half an hour.

The next night, October 6, at the Capitol in Car-diff, Richard was told not to overrun because it was a Sunday, there were two houses and a curfew of 10pm. Richard could've cared less. Keith Richards in his 2011 autobiography said:

Little Richard's stage presentation was outrageous and brilliant. You never knew which way he was go-ing to arrive. He had the band thumping out 'Lu-cille' for almost ten minutes, which is a long time to keep that riff going. The whole place blacked out, nothing to see but the Exit signs. And then he'd come out of the back of the theatre. Other times he'd run on stage and then disappear again and come back. He had a different intro almost every time. What you realized was that Richard had checked the theatre, talked to the lighting people,

'Where can I come from?' 'Is there a doorway up there?'...and figured how he could get the most effective intro possible: whether it's bang, straight in or whether to let the riff roll for five minutes and then turn up from the loft. You're not just playing a club where presentation means nothing and there's no room to move. ...And after all, Little Richard was one of the best masters we could have learned from."[108]

The Flintstones provided backing for both Mickey Most and Julie Grant who were on the bill before sharing the stage with Little Richard. Most said of Richard:

He didn't really have an act as much as he would just go out and go berserk for half an hour. Mick Jagger spent much of the tour watching Little Richard from the wings in amazement following the moves an learning stagecraft from the master.[109]

Bill Wyman told *Record Mirror:*

Richard brought the house down when he jumped off stage, went up the centre aisle followed by members of the audience, out of the front doors, then back in through a side-exit and on stage. He partly undressed and threw pieces of clothing into the crowd. He performed way past his scheduled time and his manager had to yell to him, 'Richard, stop preaching,' to get him off." The next day Bill West who was in charge of productions at Rank Theatre told him that he must not jump off stage again. Naturally he disobeyed the order and would say, "It's the music, it just gets to me. I can't help it."[110]

Graham Knight recalled:

I remember Richard leaping off the stage and running up the centre aisle. The fans were dancing in

the aisle and blocking him in. There were no wireless mics then and so he was just hollering at the top of his voice. Eventually, Peter Grant and I got him back on stage."[111]

Mick Jagger, Little Richard, 1987

Part of Little Richard's small entourage in Europe was his Bible college friend Walter Arties IV. He started praying for Richard in Cardiff as he thought he had been possessed by the Devil. Don Arden dismissed this.

Richard always carried a bible with him, so that he could preach to people on the street. My son David picked it up and looked inside it and found that down all the margins, Richard had written the names of his lovers, along with descriptions of what they did when he shagged them. That was his message to God.

Richard, in another of many states of indecision,

told *Record Mirror* in London, "I want people to forget me as a rock 'n' roller. I'm going to be an evangelist
like Billy Graham." On this point Keith Richards, in
his autobiography, *Life,* was somewhat cynical of Little Richard's religious leanings for other reasons. He
felt that Richard was a preacher for tax purposes:

> *The Reverend Richard Penniman. Never forget he
> comes from the gospel church like most of them do. We
> all sang Hallelujah at one time or another. Al Green,
> Little Richard, Solomon Burke, they all got ordained.
> Preaching is tax free. Very little to do with God, a lot to
> do with money."*[112]

Nonetheless, as it had been with The Beatles, Richard
loved the Rolling Stones. He and Mick especially got
along because Richard loved outrageousness and Mick
was the king of it.

Richard, The Rolling Stones, Julie Grant, Bo Diddley,
Mickie Most and The Everly Brothers played the Gaumont Theatre in Watford, England Oct 5, 1963; the Capitol Theatre in Cardiff, Oct 6, 1963; the Odeon Theatre in
Cheltenham, Oct 8; and the Gaumont Theatre in Worces-
ter, Oct 9, 1963. They repeated these venues at least once
during their performance schedule.

Richard's last stop on this glorious tour of Europe
ended in a near riot provoking performance at the Paris
Olympia. It was a fitting way to end the love and adulation he received from his hardcore fans.

But he still had one more appearance to make. Don Arden had indeed put together a TV spectacular to star Little Richard which was produced by Britain's biggest independent TV company, Granada Network Ltd. *The Little Richard Spectacular* was filmed in the company's Man-chester studio, with a popular American female group the Shirelles ('*Will You Still Love Me Tomorrow?*' and '*Tonight's the Night*') as backing vocalists and Sounds Incorporated as the backing band.

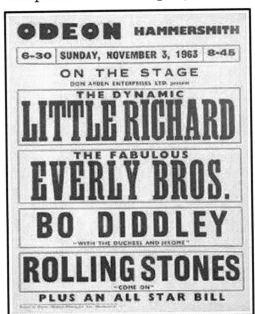

They came close to Richard's original sound and to re-creating the excitement of the Upsetters. The spectacular was aptly named. After hilarious rehearsals, during which all the musicians seemed to have a bottle of liquor stashed, filming started with Richard storming on set and straight into *Rip It Up, Lucille,* and *Long Tall Sally.* With so much power and intensity it seemed as if he might have a heart attack. But he went on with more energy the harder he worked.

He would crouch over the piano to play his driving boogie riffs, then leaped away to shout "Oooh my soul!"

"My, my, my," and "Well, all right" between numbers, bringing the young invited audience to their feet to wildly dance and clap around the studio floor. His amazing performance astounded viewers, and the show was forced to have a repeat run the next year.

At another of Don Arden's requests, after the Little Richard spectacular, Richard went straight onto another short tour featuring himself, Duane Eddy, the Shirelles, the Flintstones, Mickie Most and the Roofraisers. But Little Richard only appeared for a few dates as he apparently injured his ankle (no doubt from jumping on and off the piano so frequently) and had to return home for medical treatment. I say "apparently" because he *sailed* home, a bizarre decision for someone in pain.

Twelve

The British Are Coming! The British Are Coming!
1964

Once back in Los Angeles in late November 1963, Little Richard returned to giving sermons to the public. Don Everly of the Everly Brothers was in a supermarket one day and happened to find Little Richard preaching in there. Richard told him, "England is going to be one of the first places I will visit in passing on the word of God."

But it wasn't.

Clearly Richard was having another crisis of conscious struggling again between God and Rock. He recorded a song for Art Rupe and Specialty Records called *Bama Lama Bama Loo* in hopes it would bring him back into the American mainstream Rock & Roll consciousness after a second triumphant European tour. This time when Richard returned from Europe his new task was to set about trying to duplicate this success in the U.S.

But later that month, the country was plunged into mourning. On November 22nd, President John F. Kennedy was assassinated. Richard cried. The President was so young with a beautiful wife and two small children. For Richard, JFK was a symbol of hope for African Americans. Kennedy had been elected due in part because he helped get Dr. Martin Luther King out of Reidsville prison where King had been arrested for violating the state's anti-trespass law, and three days later incarcerated in Reidsville prison for violating the terms of his one-year suspended sentence, and $25 fine for driving without a proper permit the year before.

As a result of Kennedy's efforts, black voters turned out in record numbers and voted for Kennedy who was elected by a narrow margin of only 100,000 votes over Richard Nixon. Kennedy was also putting forth civil rights legislation he intended to see through into law. Now Kennedy was dead in a racist 1963, and Richard wondered what was to happen?

The country, in fact the world, was in deep state of depression and sadness. No one could function as the drama played out when Lee Harvey Oswald, who'd had a hand in the plot to assassinate Kennedy, was apprehended, then himself assassinated three days later on live television, and finally JFK's lying-in-state and ultimate funeral. Everything just seemed to stop.

Additionally, Richard was also affected by the deaths of W.E.B Du Bois, and Patsy Cline that year, as well as missing his friends Buddy Holly, Ritchie Valens and the Big Bopper who died in a plane crash, and Eddie Cochran with whom he toured.

By February 1964, Americans were still in mourning and needed to be revitalized. Young people yearned to be "all shook up" again musically because the creative excitement in Rock & Roll had been submerged in dormancy, boredom and the departure of many of its stars from the scene.

Elvis joined the army and was gone for two years— and when he returned he was devoid of his sideburns and singing ballads and hymns; Chuck Berry was serving 20 months in prison for violating the Mann Act for transporting a fourteen-year-old girl across state lines for allegedly "immoral" purposes; the music industry was shuddered by scandals over payola; and Jerry Lee Lewis was engulfed in controversy after bigamously marrying his thirteen-year-old cousin."

Add to this, 1964 brought disappointing news for Richard. His recording for Art Rupe, *Bama Lama Bama Loo* had tanked. Though it reached #6 in the U.K., it only reached #82 on Billboard's pop chart where it died a slow death. Richard was devastated. This record was supposed to help him get back to where he once belonged. But according to all, it missed that mark because Richard was a little bit older (at 32 no less!) and a little less wild.

While he had been touring Europe in the previous two years, the Architect of Rock & Roll had become a tough act to sell to a new American audience of rebellious youth. Now Richard felt he must go back to preaching—an act to take another musical star from the heavens.

As was always the case, just as he made up his mind to don his priestly robes again, he found himself that February watching the Ed Sullivan show, and there in front of him was his former opening act—The Beatles—singing to hordes of screaming young white girls while employing Richard's own "Wooooo's."

Little Richard had yet to be invited on the Ed Sullivan Show, yet the Beatles were being given three successive weeks of visual promotion on his show while their albums sold into the millions. It would be the same for the Stones, the Kinks, and the Who. All million seller acts utilizing Richard's unique performance tactics. The very groups who had opened for him in Europe, hit the United States and became so popular it was called "the British Invasion."

I had been out of the public's eye in America for so long they had forgotten me. It was like starting all over again like when I was just a teenage boy. I needed to break through again. Things had changed. There were all these English groups, the Beatles, the Stones, Herman's Hermits, Gerry and the Pacemakers, and they just overshadowed my thing. But I was determined to make it."[113]

As determined as Richard was to succeed and as competitive as he was, the energy and quirkiness with which he had always performed came dangerously close to becoming novelty, and the world had focused its fascination on the British invasion. Many of those groups, primarily the Beatles, who overpowered Little Richard on the charts, had become successful by melding slightly off-color lyrics with rich, sometimes unorthodox vocal effects. Along with enthusiasm and a new appearance, they presented an image that white Americans could self-identify with and, as such, they no longer needed the white and black American hybrid form to find their identities within the revolution.

Richard didn't know it then, but realized a few months later, that *he* was partially responsible for inspiring most of the bands that became 'The British Sound of the 60s."

What I have found interesting is that once the British invasion happened in the United States, Richard's own star dimmed in favor of this new sound—which was really black cadences and wails of soulful emotion emanating from white singers from the UK.

To contextualize this, consider the times in England versus those in America. The United Kingdom had always been more progressive regarding race relations than America. Yes, there was (and is) racism there, but not nearly as systemic as compared to the United States. England ceased trading in slaves in 1801 and ended slavery in 1833. America did not pass the 13th amendment and abolish slavery for another 32 years. In England, there is a large influx of Africans, Jamaicans and mixed-race citizens, and when Mick Jagger sang about "Brown

Sugar" or interracial dating, it wasn't something one was lynched for.

No one batted an eye when white British bands were publicly enamored of African American singers, and we are all too familiar with the numerous black Americans who left exclusion, ageism, and discrimination in the U.S. to become ex-Pats living and working happily in Europe where they achieved acclaim, work and continued success for their talents—the most recent being Tina Turner relinquishing her American citizenship to be a Swiss national who still enjoys her career in her 80s.

Even Richard experienced this as he was tremendously successful and maintained his success in Britain and other countries in Europe but was marginalized in his own country. Still, Richard would not give up. He had to see his Rock & Roll career through in America.

Following the flop of *Bama Lama,* Richard felt he had to do something big. Something different. He hired some musicians for a proposed weekly show entitled *The Little Richard Show*. A pilot was shot in 1964. But the project never came to light.

Finally, his old producer friend Bumps Blackwell, who was now producing Sam Cooke suggested that perhaps Richard needed to change his band's sound a bit to fit the new sound in Rock music—the use of rhythm and base guitars more so than horns.

Reminded of how Sam Cooke had taken charge of his own career, that September Richard decided to invest $16,000 of his own money to organize a new tour. He had elaborate costumes designed, found and employed background vocalists, dancers, and comedians, then utilize a band to include two guitar players.

Since acoustic guitars were not used as much except for folk singers and Richard figured in for a penny, in for a pound, he went for electric guitars. There were seventeen members altogether. Richard's plan was to be loud and gaudy, and to come back as what he called "The Living Flame"—an homage to his friend James Brown who had the business sense to finance his own tours as well.

Richard hit the road promoting his frenetically energetic comeback single, *Bama Lama Bama Loo* (even if it had failed, it was still a new song), and he chose to capitalize on the British Invasion sweeping the States, he hired a six-piece band and called them the "Crown Jewels"—three guardsmen known as "His Royal Company" (dressed in traditional Buckingham Palace uniforms, red tunics, and tall, black fur hats the Brits called "bearskins", several dancers, and a throne carrier.

Little Richard with the Crown Jewels and His Royal Company

Richard was staying at the Royal Hotel in Atlanta when he heard that Gorgeous George was in town. Gorgeous George Odell was known for his blond wigs and costumes he made himself. Richard wanted to meet the legendary black performer who, like him, dressed and performed so outrageously and a meeting was arranged. The two flamboyant men—George and Richard—had lunch after which George responded to a comment Richard made about wanting to use more guitarists in his band. George

George Odell, known as "Gorgeous George", circa 1961

said, "I want you to meet my 'cousin,' Maurice James. He plays phenomenal guitar." Richard couldn't resist George's pitch about the talented young man.

But George also told Richard that James' guitar was in hock and would require $150 to get it, and his amp, out of the pawnshop. Since George was "temporarily out of cash," he wasn't able to help his cousin. Richard gave George $175. Half an hour later the guitar player showed up. At first, Maurice—whose real name was Jimi Hendrix, an unknown at that time—didn't want to tour with Little Richard because he was scheduled to tour with Sam Cooke in a few weeks. Sam had just released *A*

Change is Gonna Come and was scheduled to do a tour promoting it. Richard asked to hear Jimi play. Jimi strapped on his guitar and that was it. Said Richard:

> *He was outrageous in his playing. You got to remember that at this time he didn't play the kind of music he played when he got famous. He was playin' blues—B. B. King type blues—he was playin' Little Richard...*[114]

Richard hired Jimi on the spot. Jimi had seen Little Richard preach in his neighborhood in Seattle and had heard his music for years. Now Jimi was about to play in Richard's band. Thinking life on the road and playing with the shocking Little Richard would allow for Jimi's own brand of flamboyant expression, the guitarist became excited and agreed to join Richard's new back-up band that included the Upsetters and the Crown Jewels.

In 1985 on the South Bank Show, Little Richard was asked what he thought of Jimi Hendrix, and Richard said "Jimi Hendrix, woooooh, Jimi Hendrix, woooooh, first time I seen Jimi Hendrix my toe shot straight up in my boot."[115]

To be fair, there are two versions of how Jimi Hendrix ended up in Little Richard's band. Jimi's version is that by the end of 1962 he had moved to Vancouver, Canada to play with Bobby Taylor and The Vancouvers. There, he met Little Richard who was in town during a stay in Vancouver. Hendrix played most weekends with Taylor and the Vancouvers until Little Richard—considered the most flamboyant and hysterically exciting of all the 50s rockers—came into Dantes Inferno Club looking for musicians. In the end, Little Richard scooped up half of Bobby Taylor's band including the lead guitarist himself. But it wasn't the first time Jimi had met the Georgia Peach. Recalls Jimi's brother Leon:

> Me and Jimi met Little Richard in 1959 because his mom and sister lived in Seattle," recalls Jimi's surviving brother Leon, speaking to Mojo Magazine. "I took a bunch of greens over to a neighbor's house, Mrs. Penniman, saw this black limo and Little Richard. I ran home to get Jimi, we rode bikes up there and sat there in awe at him preaching at the Goodwill Baptist Church."[116]

At any rate, Jimi came on board Little Richard's tour in early December 1964. Henry Nash, one of Little Richard's band members mused,

> *"I will never forget Jimi loading his belongings on the bus. His guitar was wrapped in a potato sack. It only had five strings on it. But he made a good impression on the band, though, and they welcomed having him on stage with them."*[117]

Sadly, a few days later Jimi and Little Richard were shocked by news of Sam Cooke's sudden and untimely death. On December 11, Cooke died in a motel on South Figueroa Street in the Los Angeles area of Watts, shortly after his successful engagement at the Copacabana in

New York, and his successful screen test for 20th Century Fox. He was shot and killed by Bertha Lee Franklin, a motel manager. A drunken liaison with a woman had gone wrong and Cooke's assumption that his clothes and money had been stolen and that she had fled into the motel office led Cooke to confront Franklin, who kept a .22 handgun as precaution after a series of robberies. The case was ruled "justifiable homicide" even though there is enormous suspicion and controversy over it. Little Richard and Jimi Hendrix took Cooke's death hard.

Richard was distraught because he remembered how Cooke provoked his ego forcing him to compete by not singing gospel in London in favor of his more famous Rock & Roll hits after Cooke had brought the house down. before him. If he took anything from Sam Cooke's life and now demise, it was that he had to do for himself.

So he embarked on his own self create, self-promoted tour of the United States.

Sam Cooke and Little Richard circa 1962

Thirteen

A Jimi Hendrix Experience
1965

L ittle Richard's 1965 tour promoted his new release on Specialty, *Little Richard: His Greatest Hits*, which featured twelve re-recordings of his most successful songs from the 1950s. Richard's sextet, called the Crown Jewels, featured Wade Jackson on drums, Eddie Fletcher on bass, Frank McCray and Boogie Daniels on tenor saxes, Glen Willings on rhythm guitar and "Maurice James" aka Jimi Hendrix, on lead guitar.

In Los Angeles, Richard recorded two songs with Hendrix as guitarist: *I Don't Know What You've Got (But It's Got Me)*, and *Dancing All Around the World*. Then they went out on tour which started out with 32 cities committed and more would sign on later.

On March 9, Richard appeared solo on Dick Clark's weekly music show *American Bandstand*.

Biographer Paul MacPhail described the visuals:

Richard was dressed in white shirt and white trousers with a big medallion around his neck, covered by a huge white cape and hair high and waving with the music. He sat at a baby grand piano, surrounded by three guys dressed like Buckingham Palace guards, as he faked playing piano, and lip-synced his hit, Lucille.[118]

But despite the national broadcast, Richard was still under great stress. He was having difficulty getting bookings with the shifting tastes of popular music audiences.

During some of his 1965 performances, Richard compared himself to another flamboyant dresser and eccentric pianist of the time: Liberace. The effeminate manner and dazzling costumes may have worked well in some clubs for the self-proclaimed "Bronze Liberace," but privately some of Richard's band members and road crew were mocking.

Like Gorgeous George, Little Richard wore a gaudy, shiny silver wig when he was at the Fillmore, and he sported a matching sequin jacket, silver lamé pants, and silver shoes for the concert. Jimi and the rest of the band, as usual, were relegated to wearing their obligatory uniform: white shirt, black suit, tie.

Additionally, when onstage, Little Richard did not allow anyone to outshine him either in behavior or in dress. Beautiful singer Rosa Lee Brooks, who became Hendrix's girlfriend after they met in Los Angeles

witnessed Jimi's challenge to Richard's dress code rules
during an April concert:

It was at the Golden Bear Club, in Huntington
Beach. My partner, Pat, went with me, and I did Jimi's
hair before the show. I gave Jimi a white, puffy, Errol
Flynn type of blouse to wear, with
the big sleeves and pointed collar.
I also gave him a bolero, like a
vest. Before the gig, Jimi said to
me, 'I'm going to show you something special tonight.' I wasn't
sure what he meant, but I went
along with it. He played the guitar behind his head, between his
legs, and with his cuff links.

Rosa Lee Brooks

After the gig, we were all supposed to leave together, but Little Richard called for a meeting with his
two guitar players. Glen Willings had worn a shirt that
was apparently too colorful. Jimi later imitated Little
Richard's lambasting of his and Willings's unacceptable fashion statements:

'Hendrix, you be deaf? You get rid of that shirt,
boy! Brothers, we've got to have a meeting. I am Little Richard, and I am the King of Rock and Roll, and
I am the one who's going to look pretty on stage. Will
you please turn in those shirts or else you will have
to suffer the consequences of a fine.' [119]

Little Richard also refused to let anyone, even the su-
premely talented Hendrix, outshine him onstage. That

rule applies to attire, hair, and even facial expressions. Hendrix had started to copy Little Richard but with his guitar. He began wearing make-up and bandanas in his hair which is now big and bushy. Said Brooks:

> He also started doing 20 minute solos onstage which made Richard furious—and he called another meeting and told Jimi to cut the 20 minute solos and his hair. Jimi responded that he wasn't going to cut his hair for anybody. Little Richard said, "Uh, what is this loud outburst? That will be a five dollar fine for you." Hendrix later elaborated on the dressing down he received when he wore another frilly shirt at a rehearsal. Little Richard reportedly took one look at Jimi's clothing and announced, "Shit...you fired!" Jimi was rehired the next day, after selling the shirt. [120]

Brooks could see that Jimi liked recording with Little Richard, but he let her know he was extremely uncomfortable with Little Richard's controlling behavior and sexual advances. "When I first met Jimi," she said, "he was under so much stress from being chased by Little Richard. He was ready to get away from him." Jimi and guitarist Glen Willings would make jokes about Richard's homosexuality by imitating his high-pitched voice, "'I'm Little Bitchard, and I'm the Queen of Rock-and-Roll,'" said Brooks.[121]

All jokes aside though, when he wasn't hassling Hendrix over his wardrobe, Richard was trying to get the guitarist's clothes off. The trick was for Jimi to rebuff

Richard's physical urges while not offending his boss on too many occasions. When Jimi gently made it clear that his 'jimmy' was off limits and that he was not sexually interested, Richard then asked if he could watch Jimi and Brooks have sex together. The answer was still no.

But Jimi pushed the limits with moments of fabulous musical expression and took out some supersonic revenge on Richard with his Fender guitar. There were times when Jimi whipped Richard's head around with frenzied bursts of sound. Additionally, Hendrix started to copy Little Richard but with his guitar. He began to complain about the tour saying it was "an awful experience. Plus it's bad pay, lousy living, and getting burned." "I found it difficult to contain myself," Jimi later reflected on his time with Richard. "It was okay at first, but then you get to a point when you can't stand anymore."

Then Hendrix started playing his guitar with his mouth during performances—which upset Richard to the max upon seeing it while onstage. It taught Richard an invaluable lesson about allowing himself to be upstaged. As a result, he had his lighting directors turn the lights off where Jimi was playing during the tour. When asked if in all the years he'd performed, if anybody upstaged him or took a show away from him, Little Richard categorically retorted:

Uh, yes, Jimi Hendrix. He was my guitar player, and you know, we didn't know he could play with his mouth. One night I heard this screamin' and hollerin' for *him*! I thought they were screamin' for me. But he was back there playin' the guitar with his mouth. He didn't do it again, 'cause we made sure the lights didn't come on that area no more. We fixed that! We made *sure* that was a black spot![122]

But Hendrix was not the only one who resented Little Richard's artistic totalitarianism. "Little Richard would fine us fifty dollars if we didn't call him 'King,'" said Buddy Travis. "He even fined Thomas, the captain of the Royal Company, for smiling once during a performance. They were just supposed to stand there with no expression."

It all came to a head when the tour arrived in New York. Little Richard and his revue were part of the week-long Soupy Sales Easter Show at the 3,660-seat Paramount Theater in Times Square. The lineup featured, among others, the Hollies, Shirley Ellis, the Vibrations, the Exciters, the Detergents, the Hullabaloos, the Hullabaloo Dancers, and a sixteen-piece orchestra.

Richard's first show began grandly as a belly dancer cavorted while Jimi and Glen Willings played. Richard then entered to a burst of drumbeats. Cascading down a red carpet, wearing a long, magnificent black cape, he began pounding out *Lucille* on the piano.

On the first day of the Paramount shows, Richard removed his shoes and tossed them out to his screaming admirers. When they begged for more, he began removing more items of clothing under the privacy of his cape and flung them to young girls who fought madly to grab a piece of them.

In his autobiography, Soupy Sez! comedian Sales explained how the trouble began:

> The show lasted more than three hours and we were doing five shows a day, which was insane. So, the promoter of the show called us in after the first show and he said to us, " ... *Cut down your act to ten minutes, because we've got so many acts in the show.*" And then he turned to me and said, "*Soupy, you can do fifteen, eighteen minutes, whatever you like.*" ... What I didn't know was Little Richard got very upset, because he thought I said I didn't want him to do more than ten minutes. [123]

Richard did not appreciate promoter Morris Levy's decision to shorten the acts of everyone except Soupy Sales, even though Sales was the biggest draw. Richard felt *he* was the top performer on the bill and made his feelings clear, with the moral support of Jimi Hendrix.

But Richard did not know nor consider who he was dealing with. Morris Levy was the owner of Roulette Records and had booked the Paramount Theatre for the next year. He was also Mob connected and not about to have *any* performer make demands of him. This is the man who forced his name onto songwriting credits of many of his recording artists, like Frankie Lymon, to unjustly gain additional publishing monies—and in reality Little

Richard's section of the Paramount show had run long prior which prompted warnings from Levy.

Furthermore, Richard, who had recorded on Roulette Records, was under the impression *he* was the headliner, not Soupy Sales. Whether Levy deceived Richard in order to sign him for the show is unclear, but Richard felt insulted by Levy's decision to give Sales more time on stage.

> I was very, very mad. He wanted Soupy to close the show. Me and Morris Levy got into a fight. He got mad with me and Jimi Hendrix and he told me, 'You'll find yourself floating in a lake.' I never heard that before, so I called him a black dog. And when I said 'black dog,' he leaped up from behind that desk. I didn't know Morris could jump that high.[124]

Theater manager Bob Levine described the action during a later performance that sealed the coffin on Richard's fate at the Paramount.

> Little Richard did about ten minutes or so, but then turned to the audience and said, *'Management doesn't want me to play any more music. How do you feel about that?'* The crowd of course went wild and he continued to perform, running over his scheduled time. We immediately closed the curtains and had the house band play over him. Richard stormed off the stage in a fit of rage. Things got out of hand, and one of the stagehands called the cops.[125]

The Animals, in New York shooting an episode of NBC's pop show *Hullabaloo,* went to the Paramount to see Little Richard's appearance. Lead singer Eric Burdon was riding up the elevator with Richard and witnessed an argument in which he said Richard, "with his high-pitched voice, sounded like an old woman gone berserk." He recounted it in Vanity Fair magazine in 2002:

> [T]here was a huge fight backstage at the Paramount Theater in New York between the manager of the Paramount and our publicist. Little Richard's set kept going overtime, and they were going to slap him with a $10,000 fine, and he was just going off: "I am Little Richard, I am the king!"—emulating Cassius Clay. And there was this little black kid running around, toweling him down and trying to get him to cool down. And that turned out to be Jimi Hendrix.[126]

Bobby Taylor, drummer of the Hollies, witnessed his hero Little Richard restrained in an arm lock with a gun at his throat screaming, *"Those little white girls out there love me!"* inside the elevator. Taylor continued:

> It was quite a tantrum. Richard seemed oblivious to the fact that the burly cop restraining him had a gun pressed into his neck while he carried on with his loud protestations. Fortunately, the trigger wasn't pulled.[127]

British journalist Keith Altham, who developed an ongoing friendship with Hendrix later, continued the story:

The security officer who was in the lift drew his gun, stuck it under Little Richard's chin, as if to say, 'If you don't shut up, I'm going to blow your head off.'" ...The lift stopped ... and Chas Chandler got out with Jimi... to avoid the furor that was going on in the lift. Just before Richard was tossed out of the theater, he said, 'I'll get even with Soupy.'[128]

Richard was slapped with a fine and the incident was reported in the newspapers. In an article in the May 1, 1965 issue of *The Pittsburgh Courier* Richard was quoted:

They wanted me to cut my act to six minutes. I take that long just to warm up. It was an insult to me as an artist." Then Morris Levy said: *"Richard was un-cooperative from the start. We had a long show, and to give every act a chance to get on and do its stuff, we limited all of the acts time.*

The article adds that: Little Richard indicated that he will file a suit against Levy's firm, unless he gets paid his $3,500 for the 10 days, although he only played two."

But in the end, Little Richard's operation was bleeding cash, and everything had been going wrong from the beginning. It started out alright in September 1964 when the tour was first put together, but by May 1965, Richard's accountant calculated it was costing $12,000 per week to maintain the extravagant production. As a result, many venues couldn't afford his show and bookings were declined. Producer Art Rupe tried to revive Richard's career: "He came back and did a few sides for us, one of which was 'Bama Lama Bama Loo' the result of which was a disaster."

It was clear that Richard was on the downward side of his career, and it was unlikely that Jimi would continually hold back his resentment at playing Richard's music and playing by

Little Richard Stayed Onstage Too Long, Fired

NEW YORK CITY, N. Y.— Because he "stayed on stage too long," colorful "Little" Richard found himself out of a job, last week, at the Paramount Theatre, during an Easter Week show, headed by "Soupy" Sales, TV star.

The big-time rock 'n' roll star, who first came to fame almost a decade ago, singing "Long, Tall Sally," and "Tutti Fruitti," then quit to become an evangelist for the Seventh Day Adventist Church, visibly, "was shaken up" by his dismissal. Blaming it on professional jealousy of other acts on the bill, he said:

"They wanted me to cut my act to six minutes. I take that long just to warm up. It was an insult to me as an artist."

Morris Levy, president of Roulette Records, and the

Paramount promoter, declared that, "Richard was uncooperative from the start. We had a long show, and to give every act a chance to get on and do its stuff, we limited all of the acts' time."

"Little" Richard indicated that he will file a suit against Levy's firm, unless he gets paid his $3,500 for the 10 days, although he only played two. At one time, during the height of his career, he commanded a salary of $5,000.

When the call came to him, from God, he said, while on an Australian tour, eight years ago, he threw $15,000 worth of rings into the river, stopped processing his hair and turned to the Bible. But the lure of the crowd, and the feel of those big bills, caused him to return.

Richard's rules as a guitar-playing sidekick. Besides, the Paramount scuffle between Richard and the armed officer could have resulted in Richard or Jimi being shot and/or killed.

Because Richard's shows weren't profitable, bandmates eventually found themselves locked out of their rooms at Harlem's Hotel Theresa during a weeklong performance at the Apollo. According to Robert Penniman,

Little Richard's brother and tour manager, Jimi was fired
after playing they played the Apollo Theater:

> He was a damn good guitar player," recalled Robert,
> "but the guy was never on time. He was always late
> and flirting with the girls. . . . It came to a head in
> New York, where we had been playing at the Apollo,
> and Hendrix missed the bus for Washington, DC. I
> finally got Richard to cut Hendrix.[129] [130]

Richard felt upset when he realized Jimi had left for
good and would not be coming back. But Jimi and Willings weren't alone in being paid late. Other members on
the 1965 tour felt cheated, too. "Little Richard didn't pay
us either," said Buddy Travis. "He was supposed to pay
us $40 a night, but that soon grew to $1,500 that he owed
us. After we played Newport, Kentucky, I grabbed a wire
coat hanger, and I was going to stab Richard if he didn't
pay us our money. Robert Penniman stepped in and
stopped the scuffle, and Richard ended up giving us
$400, but he didn't let us back on the tour bus."

Clearly, Hendrix was too independent to stay with the
show for long. But despite the disagreements, sexual
tension, and false firings, Richard paid Jimi a compli-
ment:

> "He was the greatest guitar player I ever had. Not one
> of my men has ever come close to him..." Later Hen-
> dricks would say, "I want to do with my guitar what
> Little Richard does with his voice."[131]

Jimi Hendrix died at age 30, a mere six years after he left Little Richard's band. But in his short life, he indeed became one of the greatest electric guitarists in rock history. Perhaps Richard overplayed himself with the two musicians who became most noteworthy for having played in his band—Billy Preston and Jimi Hendrix—but then, as Hendrix once said of his one-time boss:

"Richard may call himself 'little,' but he has a Rushmore-sized ego."[132]

Fourteen

Whole Lotta Shakin' Goin' On
1965 - 1968

Little Richard continued to tour in 1965 and was getting more and more exhausted and frustrated. He finally got a break when his old friend Brian Epstein called and asked him to headline a series of concerts at London's Saville Theatre. Richard would be on the bill with the Quotations, the Alan Price Set, and a new group called Bluesology who would open the show. The keyboardist was a young man from Pinner, in the county of Middlesex, England named Reginald Dwight who showed promise.

Since Richard's show was the hottest ticket around, there was no shortage of newspaper, magazine coverage or television appearances for the outrageous star. It brought a lot of attention to the show and its lesser-known bands—including Bluesology. Each night when Little Richard went on Reginald Dwight would grin from backstage as he watched Richard's performance and the audience's reaction to it. Richard always opened with *Lucille* and at some point his foot went up on the piano, or he played standing up, or jumped onto the piano sashaying. Dwight was impressed. After Richard's tour de force performance on the BBC's premiere rock program singing, *I Need Love*, Epstein booked him a recording session at EMI's Abbey Road Studios made famous by such recording artists as Caruso, and the Beatles. Richard's track *Get Down With It* became the one everyone was happy with.

Once more, Richard had triumphed in Europe. And the young Bluesology piano player from Pinner, England? He went solo and changed his name to Elton John. Elton has given many an interview where he says,

> *"When I saw Little Richard standing on top of the piano, all lights, sequins and energy, I decided there and then that I was going to be a Rock 'n' Roll piano player."*

Richard loved being a huge, popular draw in Europe—even if his fame was starting to wane in America. He still had hopes to be back on top where he had been seven years earlier. But when he returned to the States, it was the same-old, same-old.

As a result, Richard began a game of musical chairs regarding record label signings. It started when he signed with Modern Records and released a modest charter, *Do You Feel It?* He then left Modern for Okeh Records in early 1966. Two poorly produced albums followed which were released over the year—one of them a live album cut at the Domino, in Atlanta, Georgia.

Okeh tried everything, even pairing Richard with his old friend, Larry Williams, an American R&B and rock & roll singer, songwriter, producer, and pianist from New Orleans. Williams was best known for writing and recording some rock and roll classics from 1957 to 1959 for Specialty Records, where he and Richard met. Williams was then introduced to Bumps Blackwell, Specialty's then house producer, and was signed to record.

When Richard bolted from rock & roll to pursue the ministry, Williams was quickly groomed by Blackwell to replicate Richard's success. Using the same raw, shouting vocals and piano-driven intensity, Williams scored with a number of hit singles.

Now, Williams was producing two albums on Richard, including the studio release, *The Explosive Little Richard*, which produced the low charting *Poor Dog* and *Commandments of Love*. His second Okeh album, the aforementioned, *Little Richard's Greatest Hits Recorded Live!* returned Richard to the album charts, but it, too, tanked.

By 1967, the second year of his contract with Okeh Records without a bona fide hit single, Richard tore up his contract. According to him, because the label was a black-owned R&B label, they wanted him to sing in a more R&B style. After numerous disputes over what material to sing and the musical direction of his career, he walked out on the label. Richard then signed with Brunswick Records. But that same year he left the label equally dissatisfied. So he went out on the road.

Then Richard went on a grueling tour schedule. He crisscrossed the country doing private gigs, one-nighters or multiple shows. As example; he played Isy's Supper Club in Vancouver, British Columbia from July 15 – 17; then the Red Carpet Lounge in Chicago from July 21 – 23; then The Whisky A Go-Go in St. Paul, Minnesota from July 25 – 30. He went to Las Vegas and played the Eden Roc Hotel from August 1 – 8; then it was San Diego, California at Club from August 9 – 20; and on to the Soul City Club in Dallas, Texas from August 22 - 31.

This painful schedule from Redwood City to Greensboro to Hazel Park, West Covina, San Francisco, Long Island, Washington, D.C., etc., went on for the rest of the year and Richard was exhausted.

Also frustrated. He began to feel that producers on his labels were not working to promote his records during this period. Later, he claimed they kept trying to push him toward records similar to Motown and that he wasn't treated with appropriate respect.

Since the music had changed, labels were more comfortable with him at least attempting Rhythm & Blues versus Rock, since (as stated before) Rock was inexplicably becoming a white musical genre.

Additionally, Richard's flamboyant look, while a hit in the 1950s and Europe, failed to help his labels promote him to more conservative black record buyers. Richard also claimed that his decision to "backslide" from his ministry, led religious clergymen to protest his new recordings. Making matters worse was Richard's insistence on performing in front of integrated audiences at a time of the black liberation movement. This was shortly after the Watts riots prevented many black radio disk jockeys in certain areas of the country, including Los Angeles, from playing his music. Equally fueling this was the Civil Rights and the Black Power Movements.

The Black Panther Party had heightened the consciousness of most African Americans. They wanted justice and equality in all things—not unlike Richard and his black peers in the music business wanted for themselves regarding their music, contracts and payment for their efforts vis-a-vis their white counterparts.

"Black is beautiful" was the cry of the land, and Black people wanted music about change, about times being better, about taking control. The Black Power movement advocated equal rights, fair housing, integrated schools and a call to arms for protests and demonstrations in the streets. Black folks wanted "Issue" music not "popcorn" music.

Richard found himself behind the eight ball squeezed between his mostly white fanbase who loved him—especially in Europe, and his African American audience urging him to declare his musical blackness and be socially and ethnically relevant—if he wanted their continued support. Said Richard:

> ...See, in the South the R&B stations wouldn't play my stuff because of pressure from preachers who hated show business and couldn't forgive me for giving up the ministry. And on the West Coast, especially in LA after the Watts riots, colored DJs wouldn't play my stuff because I've always been an artist for all the people and not just the blacks. ...[B]ut if your white audience is gray-haired and thick-waisted and has no interest in your new stuff, in a sense you have no audience at all."[133]

As black musical tastes evolved in the 60s and 70s, Richard was either involved in the church (he continued to "repent" and would return to gospel throughout his career) or capitalizing on the 50s sound which had become passé. As a result, his appeal was not only static but remained white as the audience for his music defined itself largely as the nostalgia crowd.

> I was always supported by white people. James Brown was different from me. He was big in the black market. When he came to town, you could get ten thousand blacks. When I came to town, you could get ten thousand whites, and about ten blacks. When I would go to Madison Square Garden, I'd have about thirty-five thousand whites and about fifty blacks in the audience. In the whole place.[134]

Finally, 1968 came in as a year to remember. Social and political changes, deaths, and the Vietnam war brought emotional tumult for Richard, but eventually success. Vietnam was on everyone's mind and demonstrations were ongoing all across the country. In February, the U.S. State Department announced the highest U.S. casualty toll of the Vietnam War, with 543 Americans killed in action and 2,547 wounded during the previous week. Bob Dylan, who had become a friend of Richard's, was singing protest songs, *Like a Rolling Stone, Blowin' in the Wind,* and *The Times They Are A'Changin'.*

But also in February, Richard's friend, former teen sensation Frankie Lymon overdosed on heroin and died at age 25. Richard found it "a tragic, wasted death."

Then, embattled President Johnson surprised everyone on March 31st in a televised address to the nation by announcing: *"I shall not seek and I will not accept the nomination of my party as your president."*

Though he was still touring, Richard struggled to be relevant in these tempestuous times and find labels that would keep him in the category he originated. So Richard found himself on yet another backbreaking schedule of performance dates. He was determined people would remember and appreciate him.

He had managed to perform in huge venues overseas in England and France but was now performing in these small venues and clubs across America. Yes, England had embraced Little Richard because to the British he was an "exotic American Negro." But sadly for Richard, America continued to put race ahead of art and it made life very difficult for him.

By 1968, I'd sold over 32 million records internationally. But the music was changin'. I had all these screaming white kids buyin' records an' loving my music in Europe, but the chart toppers here were folks like Marvin Gaye, The Temptations, The Miracles. It was all Motown and Stax Records. Black R&B."

Richard and his music were almost considered dated and corny, and he was left with nowhere to go. He wanted to find a way to process what was happening in the news into his music in the way Bob Dylan had used world events to inspire his own lyrics. But Richard's sensibilities were not political musically. They were rhythmic, feel-good tunes.

Now acting as his manager, since Bumps Blackwell was producing so many acts these days, Larry Williams convinced Richard to forget recording for the moment and focus on live shows.

Williams used his influence to book an unexpected show for Richard in Las Vegas. It was a two-week engagement at The Aladdin Hotel in March 1968. The Aladdin was a huge venue and had never had a rock act in there before. Little Richard was in fact a replacement for the act they had actually booked who became ill. So, this unexpected opportunity could change the game for Little Richard and move the needle forward the way he wanted.

Richard decided that for this gig he'd pull out all the stops and adapt a wilder flamboyant, androgynous look, inspired by the success of his former backing guitarist Jimi Hendrix. At his first show he wore a red jacket with tiny mirrors on it, and when he strutted out he just stood there and let the audience go crazy with the light show his costume created. By his second show the line of people wanting to see Little Richard was all the way through the casino. People couldn't get to the gambling tables. He broke house records. Since they had originally planned on two shows a night, they had to up it to three to accommodate the huge crowd hungry to see Richard's show and he had them dancing in the aisles.

The Aladdin management did a bit of some juggling and asked Richard to stay on for another two weeks—for which Richard happily complied.

But a crisis exploded on April 4th. Richard was in his dressing room at the Aladdin when a band member ran in and told him the news. He turned on the television in the room and there was the newsflash from Chet Huntley:

"Dr. Martin Luther King was assassinated in Memphis and pronounced dead moments ago."

Everything was now almost in slow motion. Anger, grief, frustration and disbelief engulfed Richard. Band members were in tears. No one knew what to do. Riots had erupted all over America—but Richard chose to go on. To be onstage where he felt his music could be of benefit to a crowd in utter depression. He had to go on—to entertain, to help people forget for two hours that student activism had swept the globe, that there were mass demonstrations in Poland, West Germany, Mexico City, Paris, Italy and elsewhere, and that unrest in America and across the globe in southeast Asia did not let up.

Richard's three shows at the Aladdin were packed. Yes, everyone was angry, spirits were low, and African Americans in particular were enraged and dejected—including Richard. But at one point he acknowledged Dr. King's death and he and the audience had a moment of silence. Then the Architect of Rock & Roll closed out his show with a gospel song to mesmerize everyone there.

Fifteen

Festivals, Egos and Lennon

Obviously custom-made for Vegas, Little Richard was booked into several two-week stints at the Aladdin and in Reno in 1968. Then he appeared on the *Pat Boone Show,* the *Joey Bishop Show,* the *Tonight Show Starring Johnny Carson* and the *Della Reese Show.* He was even the subject of a ABC TV's *Music Scene* episode.

But as Richard began to rise again, he felt he and Bumps Blackwell were not communicating well. According to Richard, Blackwell began to shout at him and was "nasty" as he tended to be when Richard was enjoying success and the money he was making. Richard fired Blackwell, and let Larry Williams go. Out of the blue, he hired J.W. Alexander, Sam Cooke's old manager. Quite naturally Blackwell was upset and Alexander astonished. Alexander welcomed the opportunity to manage Richard but was always skeptical. He and Blackwell had both worked together in the old days at Specialty Records where Alexander was an A&R man as was Blackwell. He didn't want any untidy feelings between he and Richard's now former manager, so he was cautious. Blackwell considered suing but thought better upon the realization it would not be worth it financially.

Alexander took over while Richard was still in Las Vegas at his second two-week run at The Aladdin. He made it possible for Richard to get back in the Local 47 union and got Richard signed with the Associated Booking Corp of New York. Richard started to work in Baltimore, Vancouver, Indiana, Chicago and Detroit and stayed busy throughout the rest of April and May.

But on June 1st, the night before his third engagement at the Aladdin, Richard shocked everyone once again by announcing he had fired J.W. Alexander as his manager and re-signed with Bumps Blackwell. Obviously the real magic for Little Richard was his working with Bumps. Knowing Richard as well as he did, Blackwell welcomed his friend and client back and immediately went to work to capitalize on Richard's long needed success.

On June 5th Richard was performing at Isy's Supper Club in Vancouver, British Columbia when news came that Democratic presidential hopeful, Robert F. Kennedy was shot and killed in Los Angeles by a young Jordanian immigrant Sirhan Sirhan. Once again the country was hurled into a state of depression. In the wake of RFK's assassination, the Democratic National Convention opened that August and thousands of demonstrators, students, antiwar activists, Yippies, Students for a Democratic Society (SDS) and the Black Panthers— poured into Chicago. They were met with a violent police response called out by Mayor Richard Daley. TV cameras captured the bloody clashes between police and demonstrators.

Richard took two days off and made some decisions. He got rid of the Upsetters for a new backup band, the Crown Jewels, some of whose members had performed with him in the 1964 version of the band like Eddie Fletcher. They performed together on the Canadian TV show, *Where It's At*. Richard felt his "feel good" music was much needed in this time of great crises and depression and was insistent on more live dates. He was accommodated by numerous engagements for the rest of the year.

Fifteen performances in Mexico City, Mexico at the Terrazzo Casino Nightclub followed in August, 1968, along with a stellar performance on August 17th in New York City with the Crown Jewels for the Central Park Music Festival at the Wollman Rink sponsored by the Schaefer Brewing Company. These performances were followed by appearances in Chicago at the Cheetah Club; the Penthouse Club in Seattle, Washington; Isy's Supper Club in Vancouver, British Columbia; the Mad Russian Club in Boston; the Whisky A-Go Go in Atlanta;

and another stint in Las Vegas at the Aladdin Hotel. Richard then closed out the year at the Hollywood Palladium.

When the new year arrived with Richard Nixon newly minted as President, Little Richard was on his way to a spectacular year. He was featured on the Monkees TV special *33⅓ Revolutions per Monkee* in April 1969, and twelve days after Neil Armstrong and Buzz Aldrin took mankind's initial steps on the moon, Richard was booked in the Atlantic City Pop Festival, a smaller but significant gathering of the hippie tribes that took place before the Woodstock rock festival immortalized upstate New York.

Held at the Atlantic City Racetrack in Mays Landing, N.J., from August 1-3, 1969, Richard would wow the house and remind everyone why he was the Architect of Rock & Roll. Filling in for Johnny Winter, Richard played his set on a white grand piano and rocked the track as he invited the audience to come up and dance on stage.

Richard was electric, had the crowd in the palm of his hands from the first *a whop-bop-a-lu"* said Larry Magid [the Electric Factory Concerts principal who booked the show]. "He jumped off his piano. He stripped off his spangly shirt. He went down on his knees to pray.[135]

"One of the best performances I've ever seen," said Herb Spivak [another organizer of the festival and senior partner of Electric Factory Concerts].[136]

Richard closed the Atlantic City Pop Festival, following a stunning performance by Janis Joplin. It was raining hard but Richard started out screaming *Lucille* and drove the audience crazy. Somehow he managed to steal the show from headliner Janis Joplin, whom he eventually invited onstage. Richard ended up throwing $3,000 worth of clothes and shoes to the frenzied crowd that night. He was that good.

After New Jersey, there was a booking in Central Park, then Richard played for 32,000 people at Madison Square Garden where he scored another success.

Then came the Toronto Peace Festival—the ultimate coup de grâce. It was September 13, 1969. Little Richard had been asked to appear along with Jim Morrison, the Doors and the Chicago Transit Authority, in front of an audience of long-haired, drug-high hippies on the stadium field who had come to protest the war in Vietnam. It was like Little Richard hailed from another era. And, in a way, it was true. Richard hadn't had a hit in ten years, and to blatantly state it, cultural taste had changed. It was the difference between *Mary Poppins* and *Easy Rider*.

The traditional rock & roll that Richard (and others) shaped was clearly on the wane which Richard knew. But he had just blown away the crowd at the Atlantic City Pop Festival two months earlier, and he was ready to do the same again.

Plus, there were other rockers appearing like his old pals Bo Diddley, Chuck Berry, and Jerry Lee Lewis, ready to take classic rock & roll to the top of the pop. Some of the more hip were even beginning to champion the old stuff, perhaps providing the first very distant glimmers of punk rock.

The show was billed as a "Rock & Roll revival," and is now considered as the first—a trend which would explode later in the early '70s. Its organizers had booked big-time rock & roll fan John Lennon who had been invited simply to host the show.

But literally at the last minute he decided he wanted to play. Lennon rounded up a few heavyweight rock friends—Eric Clapton, Klaus Voorman, future Yes drummer Alan White and Yoko Ono— to play as the Plastic Ono Band.

The problem was, it would upset the billing. Little Richard would have to play before Lennon. Richard was furious—his ego wounded. Remember, Little Richard needed to be the headliner like he needed air to breathe. John Lennon knew that Richard was the superior singer and his mentor, but his own ego was in the way. Lennon was a Beatle. A genius. A trailblazer who had just announced that day he was leaving the iconic group to go solo. He couldn't go on before Little Richard—a blast from the past.

So when talks with Lennon failed (they say Lennon threw up after leaving Richard's dressing room), Richard vowed to scorch some earth before the bearded Beatle got on stage. Lennon, who had ripped off so much from Little Richard (among others), in his journey of winning previously incredible honors, power, riches, and fame simply refused to give up the closing position.

So Richard prayed to be in superior voice and energy. Clearly, it was granted to him. The show began when Richard struts out with his outrageous pompadour and pencil mustache, face slathered in makeup, and re-splendent in a brilliant white vest covered in little square mirrors. Only when he asks for the stage lights to be turned off and the spotlight beamed on him alone did one realize his outfit was part of the light show. He was a human mirror ball with luminous flickers of light flash-ing behind him.

Then Richard and his Crown Jewels launched into *Lu-cille* in a frantic pace, his horn players in baby-blue suits nodding in syncopation to the beat.

Next came *Good Golly Miss Molly* with Richard offer-ing a powerful burst of bawdiness as he jumped up on the piano, beaming a 1,000-watt smile, shaking his mon-eymaker, and holding up his fabulous white go-go boots for all to see. He threw one into the audience, then really milked it taking his sweet time to throw the second boot. It was great showmanship. *"Ladies and gentlemen, you are looking at the true rock & roll! The 1956 rock & roll!"* he hollered proudly.

After that, he got the ladies in the crowd to scream "Wooooo!" and the men to scream "Huh!" His intent was to really eclipse and outdo John Lennon forever.

Rip It Up was shameless—and brilliant. During *Jenny, Jenny* Richard brought people up from the audience. Then came a hypersonic *Long Tall Sally*. It was a nine-song, 28-minute set. One of rock & roll's greatest live performers—the one and only Little Richard—had just pulled out all the stops. Imagine trying to follow that.

Lennon would pay dearly for his faux pas and was understandably nervous: it was the first time he'd played on stage in three years, essentially the first time he'd ever played live without at least one of the other Beatles, and his band had only rehearsed once, acoustically, on the plane to the show. Now they were going to play in front of 20,000 people with huge expectations and go on *after* Little Richard who had just wiped the audience out with his barn-burning best.

Lennon did so much cocaine before his performance that he threw up—again. It was a sorrowful sight when he played a few rock & roll hits but simply could not compete.

When his wife Yoko came on and started her set people booed, and the Doors refused to come on until things calmed down. That took an hour.

All anyone could talk about thereafter was Little Richard, and these two successes brought Richard to talk shows such as the *Tonight Show Starring Johnny*

Carson, and the *Dick Cavett Show*, making him a major celebrity all over again.

From the outside, it seemed America was finally appreciating the musical genius that was Little Richard. Still, as Richard continued to record, success on vinyl was not as automatic as it had once been for him and he found himself relegated to the nostalgia circuit. At least he scored enormous successes there, but he felt he was put "out to pasture" too early. Richard would spend the remainder of the decade "in a continual unsuccessful comeback," at least compared to his former dominance.[137]

Sixteen

The Rockin', Sockin' Seventies

In 1970, Little Richard and the Crown Jewels appeared in the Wollman skating Rink in Central Park during the summer. He really tore it up. The Schaefer Brewing Company who promoted the Wollman Rink concert described Little Richard's costume & style: *"No psychedelics. Just straight, low-down funk."* His effect was magnetic. You could not really call it a comeback because most of the kids who were there had never seen him when he first appeared, and many were not even born then. But it was a revival, a spontaneous generation of rocking pneumonia.

For the first show he came out in a red velvet suit with a gold embroidered jacket, prancing up and down like an exhibitionist talking to the kids, posing to let women take his picture, throwing kisses, camping it up, and instantly taking off his clothes, "You want my vest?" he'd say, then he'd take it off and throw it into the audience.

Continuing with his dualistic desires, Richard spent much of the 70s trying to return to the recording business at the top of the mountain while the demands of the road and his identity issues kept him racing from rock & roll to gospel and back again.

Little Richard was moving past the age of 45, and though he still possessed the energy to make his type of music work, he was simply no longer that fresh, unfamiliar face for an American audience looking for "something else." As in the case of other artists such as Chuck Berry, the new audience was willing to embrace the energy of an older artist's music, but they weren't willing to take on a hero cast in the image of their parents. The first Little Richard generation was now grown, and he lacked the original visual power with which to begin again with the young.

Additionally, new technologies had emerged for listening to music—first stereo 8-Track cassette cartridges, then the much smaller compact cassette tapes. Originally designed for dictation machines, improvements in fidelity led cassettes to supplant stereo 8-track cartridges, reel-to-reel tape recording and the once beloved 45's. Richard very much wanted to record new songs utilizing this technology.

But over the changing, rough and tumble years of the 70s, Richard found his success still eclipsed by his white British protégés, and he developed a fondness for alcohol

and drugs—especially co-
caine. "I remember meet-
ing up with him in London
in 1970," said Lee Angel. "I
was so shocked. In the
early days I had barely
seen him take a drink."138

In 1972, Richard en-
tered the rock and roll revival circuit, and that year,
he co-headlined the London Rock & Roll Show at Wem-
bley Stadium with fellow peer Chuck Berry where he'd
come onstage and announced himself "The King of Rock
& Roll," which fittingly enough was also the title of his
1971 album with Reprise. He told the packed audience
there to "Let it all hang out." Richard, however, was
booed during the show when he climbed on top of his piano and stopped singing; he also seemed to ignore much
of the crowd.

Then to make matters worse, he showed up with just
five musicians, and struggled through low lighting and
bad microphones.

When the concert film documenting the show came
out, his performance was considered strong, but his fans
noticed a drop in energy and vocal artistry. Two songs he
performed did not make the final cut of the film.
Whether this was due to his drug use or not, Richard's
addiction to cocaine had become critical.

I just lost it. They shoulda called me 'Little Cocaine' after that. I was sniffing so much of the stuff my addiction was costin' me $1,000 a day." "...I was one of the biggest cocaine addicts, smoking it, snorting it and whatever cocaine could do, I did. ...I used to have standards in my life and I lost all of that."[139]

By 1975, Richard also had an addiction to heroin and PCP, known as "angel dust." It affected every part of his career and personal life. He lost his reasoning and did whatever he could to use drugs.

He admitted on the British television show the *South Bank Show* starring Bill Hinton that,

Cocaine was something. It was something else. You know, it had me. And it can get you—that white sugar. I call it the white lion. He would run you out the jungle. I just couldn't do without it. Everywhere you look in my room, cocaine. It was everywhere. Everybody stayed in my room all the time because I had the coke. And if you keep coke, you will have company all the time.[140]

In an appearance on the same British TV show, Lee Angel went on to say that she was in London watching the Tom Jones show, when she saw Richard, and thought he was the loneliest man she'd ever seen in her life.

I guess when someone told him that I was looking for him he reached out to me. I flew to Los Angeles ...and at the airport twelve o'clock in the afternoon, 17 crazy looking guys got out of the limousine and Richard got out with this big red and gold outfit on and his pompadour and his makeup yelling, 'Shut up.' He was into drugs at that time. He just wasn't the person I knew anymore. He was drinking. He was doing drugs... and he was smoking PCP..."[141]

Richard's drug addiction got worse by the day, and was exacerbated by many tragedies he suffered in the 70s. In 1976, his friend Little Gus was shot in the head, then Richard also experienced the tragic death of a favorite nephew who was like a son to Richard. That tragedy was followed by the death of another of Richard's friends who was coming out of an apartment building when some boys, who mistook the light-skinned man to be white, killed him. They cut him up with a butcher knife, put his body in the trunk of their car—then disposed of the body between two buildings across town. Richard was devastated.

But it was the death of his younger brother Tony that had the most life-altering effect on the singer. Tony died of a cocaine-related heart attack at age 33 and Richard felt personally responsible.

My brother Tony said, 'Richard, I wanna borrow some money to buy a station wagon. I said, 'Tony when I get back I'll let you have it.' Instead of doing that, I met a man after the show and we went to the hotel. We went there to have a party. The next morning someone pushed a note under my door, saying: 'Your brother is dead.' He got up and watered his lawn and walked to his little boy and fell dead, my little brother. 33 years old. I said, 'Well, I think God is trying to tell me something.' I opened my Bible at 'Mark 36', where God says: 'What shall it profit a man if he should gain the whole world and lose his own soul?'[142]

The amount of money Richard promised Tony was only $200, but the lure of participating in a cocaine-and-sex party, coupled with Tony's subsequent death made Richard sick to his stomach and guilt-ridden.

He thought about his friend singer Frankie Lymon, and did not want to be found dead on a bathroom floor from an overdose. That, coupled with the fact that in 1977 he was nearly shot to death by Larry Williams—the same Williams who was once a friend, his record producer, and a de facto manager, pushed Richard over the edge.

Williams showed up with a gun and threatened to kill Richard for failing to pay his drug debts. Richard later mentioned that this was the most fearful moment of his life because Williams's own drug addiction made him wildly unpredictable.

All this forced Richard to make a decision. Chastened by too many tragedies and remorse, he poured his coke down the toilet, gave up alcohol, homosexuality and rock music, and he once again returned to Christian ministry. Said Lee Angel:

When Tony died, Richard just snapped. That was the end of all the drugs. He went into selling Bibles. I got a call, not long after, and I went up to see him in Los Angeles. It took me a moment to recognize him. The pompadour had gone. His hair was like it was when he was young.[143]

All the while, Bumps Blackwell was on the sidelines concerned and worried about Richard even though he was no longer Richard's manager. Richard had fired him—again—and hired his brother Marquette Penniman to handle management. But Blackwell was in the uncomfortable position of having to hear about Richard's drug use, his depression, and his former client's lostness.

I just didn't stick around much after that when I became aware of it, [Richard's drug use]. Because I always never went beyond the green door, I always allowed him his privacy. I ran a very clean ship all through the 50s and 60s. And it was between '73 and '74 when I thought that I didn't want to be a part of it, when they would come into my room—he was sending them in there for money that I couldn't account for where it was going. And I knew where it was going and I couldn't account for it. So I dismissed myself.[144]

Finding himself in precisely the same self-destructive mode as once before, but this time as an older man with weaker recuperative powers, Richard once more reacted abruptly and returned to the church in what appeared to be an impulsive reflex. Again, he renounced everything about his life, his music, himself, and his homosexuality. In an interview for the Los Angeles Times, he remarked,

> I was what you called in that day a freak...I was flam-boyant in every way. I'm glad I'm able to look back on it and say, 'Thank you Lord,' and go on.[145]

He reiterated his former belief that rock music was a demonic entity stemming from the Devil.

This was Richard's own revisionist history, of course, and it camouflaged the lifelong struggle he has waged with the rival pulls of rebellious rock & roll and deferential religion. In fact, it is that struggle that makes Little Richard such a fascinating character. If the struggle hadn't created such pressure in his music, then the release from that tension perhaps would not have felt as liberating.

But still, he was in a state of self-condemnation and maintained that his homosexuality was an evil of this world, not of genetic circumstances. He even suggested that his father's decision to throw him out of the house at an early age may have been the correct one.

He released the gospel album, *God's Beautiful City*, in 1979, and traveled the country representing Memorial Bibles, selling the Black Heritage volume to fans. It must be noted that even in his wildest days he carried a Bible and read and quoted from it regularly. So imagine the shock and surprise on one's face when they opened their door and saw Little Richard standing there, sans his famous get-up, offering his King James, Black Heritage, leather-bound bibles to them.

Then, that same year, Reverend Richard Penniman came out as a gay man at a revival in California saying:

"If God can save an old homosexual like me, he can save anybody."

The statement went viral for the time and must have been a thing to behold for anyone attending who witnessed it live.

Seventeen

The "Event" Continued

By 1980, Rock music was experiencing another major transformation. The once popular Rock & Roll piano pounding, saxophone pumping brand had morphed into several new and experimental genres which captivated young audiences on the radio and music television stations like MTV and VH1. Equally exciting was a new way to listen to music which was exploding into a lucrative new market called Compact Disks. CDs would eventually replace cassette tapes, albums and all vinyl.

These new music genres—disco, grunge, new wave, reggae, hard rock, heavy metal, alternative, and punk left no room for the 50s & 60s Little Richard, now an older star who, though having inspired, gave way to the fresh outrageousness of Prince, Patti Smith, Michael Jackson, David Bowie, Billy Idol, Donna Summer, Rick James, Freddie Mercury, George Clinton and Madonna's on-stage antics captured in music videos.

Richard looked around at his circumstances and became practical. He sold the Los Angeles home on Virginia Avenue next door to Joe Lewis' old home, where his mother and some of his siblings had been living for over 25 years and moved them all to a new house in Riverside, California. He then moved himself into Room 319 at the Continental Hyatt hotel on Sunset Boulevard in West Hollywood. He continued to preach, travel on the gospel circuit, and sell bibles...

...Until the unthinkable happened.

Once again Richard was faced with tragedy. One month before publication of a major new biography on him was about to drop his mother, his rock, became ill. Richard stopped his gospel tour and came home to the Riverside house to be with her.

In addition to Leva's illness, Richard was down because his career as a minister was not effective. People were not responding well to his sermons.

Sadly, on January 11, 1984 at age 71, Leva Mae Penniman asked Richard to promise her one thing—to remain a good Christian, and *"stay with the Lord."* Richard made his mother this deathbed promise—and Leva Mae passed from this earth with him holding her hand.

Richard was devastated and it took months for him to recover from mourning or the inability to move forward. He stayed in the hotel, sometimes for days on end and never left. He was committed now—to his faith and the promise he'd made to his dying mother. Would she be

disappointed in him if he strayed? Would she understand the sacrifices he made for his faith and love for
God? His willingness to do without true physical love or
sex with a partner he really desired? His longing (and
compromise) to do the right thing versus his need to sing
the music God put him on the planet to create?

These questions again plagued him because it was always a festering wound needing to be healed.

But then, he had so many festering wounds needing to be healed. One of them was financial He began
to think that perhaps turning his attentions to this
sore would help him cope with the death of his beloved
mother.

For years he had been angry that he was cheated
out of his rightful music royalties and he was demanding a reckoning. On Wednesday, August 15, 1984,
Richard and some friends organized a picket line and
protested outside of the ATV Music Corporation in
Los Angeles. Using his real name, Richard W. Penniman, he sued Specialty Records, Venice Music, their
owner Arthur N. Rupe, and ATV, a music publisher.
Specialty was Little Richard's label. Venice Music,
Specialty's songwriting arm, was bought by ATV in
1979.

Richard's attorney, Larry Allman, filed the lawsuit
alleging that the 1959 agreement Little Richard signed

waving all royalties in exchange for an $11,000 lump-sum payment, only applied to his recordings of such hits as *Long Tall Sally* and *Good Golly, Miss Molly*. It did not exempt the publishing companies from paying songwriting royalties which are usually split equally between publisher and artist.

Said Richard:

> Beginning in 1959, although I had settled my dispute with Rupe for the recording royalties on my biggest hits, he took the position that this release also covered songwriters' royalties and refused to pay me any songwriters' royalties from that day to this one. Consequently, I was forced to institute a federal lawsuit against him and his companies for the millions of dollars I say he owes me. The very thought of it is sickening to me now. He's made millions and he should owe me millions.[146]

The lawsuit was settled the following year but sadly, not in Richard's favor. So, in 1985 Richard made a deal with himself to stick a toe back in the Rock & Roll waters.

This was brought on, in part, by a successful authorized biography of Little Richard which was released that same year. Renewed interest in Richard soon followed, and he wanted to sing again. Perhaps even record.

He had also developed an interest in film appearances—a whole new adventure for his unique talents, particularly his sense of humor.

After he had fired Bumps Blackwell for the last time he hired his brother Marquette to start booking him to keep it all in the family.

Marquette persuaded Richard to reconsider his view on religion and his place in it. Perhaps Rock & Roll could be used for good—and not evil thought Marquette. So in early 1985, Marquette got Richard a deal to do the film *Down and Out in Beverly Hills* starring Richard Dreyfuss. When the film debuted, Little Richard received raves for his memorable appearance singing, *Great Gosh A'Mighty*.

A small group of acting roles made in the mid-80's would follow, and they showed what one critic called "a unique comedic timing" which was not such a surprise considering that he had consistently demonstrated such a quality in his stage performances, interviews, public appearances, and the previous films in which he appeared.

Following Richard's explosive rise and fall in the 50s and 60s, his reemergence in movies, not as a mere singer, but as a cultural icon, became noteworthy. Richard had hung in there. No longer the daunting outsider whose presence had to be subdued for fear it would frighten away the white ticket-buying public, but he began to be seen as a founder and not an anomaly.

He had survived coming out of a time when a black man could be lynched simply for being black, or for having white kids hug him or openly adore him. He had emerged victorious after being mistreated along the way—sometimes by himself as often as anyone—and not only endured but prevailed. Little Richard had created a musical world unlike any in history—one in which we still live.

All that was missing now was public recognition—and he was well on his way to receiving that.

That year, 1985, while 52-year-old Little Richard was in his room at the Continental Hyatt, he heard the announcement on television that he was an inductee along with James Brown, Elvis Presley, Ray Charles, Sam Cooke, Chuck Berry, Fats Domino, Jerry Lee Lewis, Buddy Holly, and The Everly Brothers in the freshman group of the Rock & Roll Hall of Fame. The first ceremony ever was to be held at the Waldorf Astoria Hotel in New York City, and aired on VH1 on March 20, 1986.

The Rock & Roll Hall of Fame!

This was revelatory news and Richard was excited. Yes, he had replaced his piano with a pulpit and gone was the makeup that helped make him famous. He had kissed his kinky orgies goodbye forever. The Architect of Rock & Roll would be universally and publicly acknowledged as just that—the Architect—even if he had come to Jesus.

But on October 9th of that year, Jesus almost came for the Architect.

Richard had been on a grueling tour in Britain. During the tour he recorded his first all-new album in eight years called *Lifetime Friends*. This album seemed to merge hedonist rock & roll exhibitionism and sacred Christian morality—the two disparate forces in his life. He was happy to have meaningful work, the respect of his peers, and nice money coming in.

After completing work on the album in London, he had an eleven hour flight back to Los Angeles on Oct. 8, 1985 followed by 12 hours filming on the set of NBC's hit television drama *Miami Vice* playing the character of "Reverend Marvelle Quinn"—a minister preaching the gospel against drug abuse beachside in Miami.

Richard was in the middle of a stunning Hollywood comeback. In addition to recording the album, he had made a music video, guest appearances on *The Tonight Show* starring Johnny Carson and *The Hollywood Squares,* and there was that stunning news of his being inducted into the Rock & Roll Hall of Fame as one of their first ever inductees.

On top of this, he was planning another world tour. It was a heady schedule—and he was exhausted.

While driving home on Santa Monica Boulevard from the Miami Vice set, Richard fell asleep at the wheel of his Nissan 300ZX sports car traveling 60 miles per hour.

He lost control of the car, and in one spectacular display of unexpected bad luck it SMASHED into a telephone pole on Curson Avenue.

The impact nearly killed him.

Firefighters and paramedics came and it took an hour trying to cut him from the wreckage with the Jaws of Life while Richard laid unconscious pinned between the steering wheel and front seat.

From an ambulance, Richard was rushed into an Emergency room O.R. His right leg was shattered, he had a punctured bladder, two broken ribs along with head and facial injuries.

For another perspective, Stuart Colman, a British record producer and DJ, told a story of what happened in London from his vantage at the time. They were shooting a documentary on Little Richard—who had flown to London to promote a book and to record a new album *Lifetime Friend*. The album was being recorded in a studio at Ridge Farm, a 16th century house in Surrey, England. They had been recording for a bit less that a week and were now laying laid down tracks for *Great Gosh A'Mighty* from *Down and Out in Beverly Hills*. Billy Preston flew in to record it with Richard since they co-wrote the song.

The two recorded the track in one fabulous take—a nine minute version of the song. Colman was very pleased, and everyone broke for the weekend. That Monday morning Colman came in early to make sure the studio was set up for the session.

"The session was due to start at midday. ...I was at another studio that morning. At 10 a.m. someone said to me, "We've just heard on the radio that Richard's broken his leg in a car crash." I said, "That's terrible. Did it happen in London?" and he said, "No—Los Angeles." Of course we couldn't figure out how it was physically possible for Richard to have got to L.A. in that time. Then we realized that L.A. was eight hours behind London, so he'd left late on Sunday and arrived there still on Sunday evening. ...He thought he could get over there for the weekend and be back on Monday to carry on recording. It transpired at the same time he'd been offered a walk-on part in Miami Vice and would pick up several thousand dollars for a few minutes work.

...It all fell apart when he jumped into his car. At the best of times, he's one of the world's worst drivers and of course he promptly fell asleep at the wheel. ...He piled the car into a telegraph pole and nearly killed himself. The crash was right outside NBC-TV studios, so they rushed out with the TV cameras and filmed Richard being taken out of the car. It was on that night's 6 o'clock news. He was in a hospital for three months."[147] *

Though they had 95% of the tracks recorded for the album, they still needed Richard's voice which they were not able to get for a while because Richard was in bad shape and experiencing so much pain.

---

* **NOTE:** Richard's accident did not happen in front of NBC studios. It happened on Santa Monica Blvd and Curson Avenue in West Hollywood, CA. Richard was taken to Cedar Sinai hospital.

When Richard awoke from surgery Dr. Edwin Gromis, his orthopedic surgeon, said Richard was lucky to be alive. During surgery, a steel rod was implanted in his right thigh bone which had been shattered into seven or eight major fragments requiring two operations to repair and 35 pins to hold it together. Gromis said, "His prognosis for recovery is excellent." He reported that Richard would probably remain in the hospital another week to 10 days and could resume normal activities in five to six months.

Though no alcohol was found in Richard's blood, authorities said he still may face charges of reckless driving and driving with a suspended license. Despite that, Richard stayed at Cedar Sinai another two weeks. He prayed, meditated, thanked God, and in going over his life, was grateful and appreciative to be among the living.

But his legs would never be the same again.

Eighteen

The Nineties

According to filmmaker John Waters, who interviewed Richard in 1987 for what ultimately was a doomed Playboy magazine article, Richard at the time of his accident, was still living in Room 319 at the Continental Hyatt hotel. He continued to be a grieving man. His household possessions from his last estate in Riverside were in storage or had been given to relatives. Fluffy, his dog, was staying with his sister. The piano his grandfather gave him was at his brother's, and a small staff, including a physical therapist named Madison, were attending him from day to day. He missed his mother. Richard told Waters:

> My niece is my secretary; I have two bodyguards I travel with, and a 24-hour limo. I need to get over my mother's death. I don't want to be by myself in no house. Everybody is gone at night; that's lonely. ...My mother died and I couldn't stand to look at her

bedroom any more. I'd get sick. I've always been a momma's boy.[148]

For most of his hospital recovery folk singer Bob Dylan sat by Richard's side. The two had been friends since the 60's. They talked, and sometimes Dylan played his guitar. But mostly Dylan kept Richard's spirits up.

Finally, wearing a blue and white turban and matching pajamas, Richard was one day well enough to be wheeled into the hospital conference room at Cedars with his legs elevated. A steel brace could be seen on his right leg. He gave a press conference.

As cameras incessantly clicked, Richard said he would continue preaching while pursuing film roles—as he had done when he appeared on NBC's *Miami Vice*. The ordained Seventh-day Adventist minister said preaching and singing gospel would be his primary interest, especially given what he called his "miraculous survival."

"I been walking by Him. Now I'm getting in His arms," said Richard. "I have never been at death's door. This is the first time."[149]

In his 2010 book "Role Models," in which filmmaker Waters resurrected and published his 1987 interview with Richard, the singer had commented on his deep, abiding and continuing religious faith especially during the trying time of his accident:

[JOHN:] "How about the rumour that it was Bob Dylan who converted you to Judaism on your deathbed following your accident?"

[RICHARD:] "Bob Dylan is my brother. I love him same as Bobby Darin [deceased] is my baby. I feel Bob

Dylan is my blood brother. I believe if I didn't have a place to stay, Bob Dylan would buy me a house. He sat by my bed; he didn't move for hours. I was in pain that medicine couldn't stop. My tongue was cut out, leg all tore up, bladder punctured. I

Bob Dylan in 1962

was supposed to be dead. Six feet under. God resurrected me; that's the reason I have to tell the world about it."

[JOHN:] "Are you Jewish now?" I inquire, repeating published reports that Richard had followed in the footsteps of Sammy Davis Jr.

[RICHARD:] "There's something I prefer not saying," he teases mysteriously. "I will say this. I'm a believer in the God of Abraham, Isaac and Jacob. I believe the seventh-day Sabbath is God's way."[150]

By January 23, 1986 Little Richard was still recovering from the accident and could not appear at his own induction into the inaugural Rock & Roll Hall of Fame. It had to be distressing not to be there in person after a life-time of much-needed (and far overdue) iconic recognition.

Richard sent a videotaped acceptance speech which induced a standing ovation from the star-studded audience assembled at the live taping in New York's Waldorf Astoria.

Finally, when Richard was physically able, he appeared in a full-length documentary based on his biographical book written by Charles White. It was produced by David Hinton for The South Bank Show in London. Though it was a well done documentary that included interviews with, among others, Bumps Blackwell and Lee Angel, and showcased rare footage of Richard preaching and being interviewed in a diner and in the backseat of a limo, it also revealed that the singer was still locked in his perennial tug-of-war between the Lord and the Devil. For starters, Richard wavered between preaching like an Evangelist in some segments, then appearing dressed in full leather and make-up in others.

He just couldn't help himself.

Later in 1986, Richard was able to begin a non-stop series of performances and appearances, including live concerts worldwide, recording projects, television, film, soundtracks and commercials.

After contemplating it for a long time, Richard filed a lawsuit in 1987 against Warner Brothers films. He was seeking a court ruling to support his claim that he had legal authorship of the theme song from *Down and Out in Beverly Hills*, a tune on which he shared credit with Billy Preston. The case was settled out-of-court.

But the 1980s were also a time of personal growth for Little Richard. He began to witness a very intense and necessary shift in comprehension and acceptance mounting for the LGBTQ community (originally LGBT) throughout the decade. Lesbian, Gay, Bisexual, Transgender and Queer organizations like GLAAD were growing exponentially. GLAAD, as example, then stood for the Gay & Lesbian Alliance Against Defamation. It was an American media monitoring organization founded by LGBT people which emerged to engender pride, fight bullying, bring attention to the unending violence against gays, and to limit negative, stereotypical representations of gays in media—especially the wake of the AIDS crisis of which the media then only targeted homosexuals.

In ten short years, big cities, small towns and communities all over the country began seeing the lives of their lesbian, gay, bisexual and transgender family members, friends and neighbors reflected in media outlets. These stories spurred the kinds of everyday conversations that had started to change hearts and minds.

GLAAD began to give awards for sensitivity in the media regarding depictions of gay people in film, TV and newspapers. Richard could see the tide was changing.

Little Richard was a high profile gay man whose inde-cisiveness regarding his own sexuality did not neces-sarily engender the kind of pride and acceptance which, as a role model, willing or unwilling, so many gay people wanted to identify with. In this new era of acceptance and self-esteem that was emerging, Richard could not be thought of as being on the wrong side of history.

In his interview with John Waters in 1987, Richard tried to set the record straight regarding his being gay.

> I love gay people. I believe I was the founder of gay. I'm the one who started to be so bold tellin' the world! You got to remember my dad put me out of the house be-cause of that. I used to take my mother's curtains and put them on my shoulders. And I used to call myself at the time the Magnificent One. I was wearing make-up and eyelashes when no men were wearing that. I was very beautiful; I had hair hanging everywhere. If you let anybody know you was gay, you was in trouble; so when I came out I didn't care what nobody thought. A lot of people were scared to be with me.[151]

Later Richard claimed that he had never became a fully ordained minister. Yet, he frequently invoked his office on behalf of friends and associates for weddings and funerals. He presided over the weddings of celebri-ties such as Little Steven of Bruce Springsteen's E Street band; Bruce Willis and Demi Moore at the Golden Nug-get in Las Vegas; Cyndi Lauper and David Thornton; and spoke in an official capacity at the funerals of Wilson Pickett and Ike Turner.

In March 1989, at an AIDS benefit hosted by Cher, Little Richard stood at a keyboard and for the first time in 13 years tore into a rendition of "Lucille" that brought down the house. Thankfully, this time his *re*-conversion to rock & roll did not involve a return to drug abuse.

By the 1990s, Little Richard played his old catalogue with no apparent shame or guilt, and he was now mature enough to admit out loud to his homosexuality. It would prove to be a noteworthy decade filled with accolades and awards. He was honored with a star on the world-famous Hollywood Walk of Fame in June 1990 at 6840 Hollywood Boulevard, and he also presided over the unveiling of "Little Richard Penniman Boulevard" in Macon, Georgia.

Then in 1993, he was honored to sing for the Inaugural Gala of William Jefferson "Bill" Clinton as President of the United States. President Clinton had personally requested he perform *Good Golly, Miss Molly*. This was truly a banner moment for Richard who never declared publicly or made any political statements in his life for want of a universal audience. To perform for a United States President was a career highlight indeed.

Also in 1993, Richard would receive the Lifetime Achievement Award from the National Academy of Recording Arts and Sciences (Grammy), followed by the Rhythm & Blues Foundation's Pioneer Award.

All these honors in recognition of his achievements made Richard comfortable enough to make a public declaration in Penthouse magazine on par with the statement he'd made at that revival in 1979:

> I've been gay all my life and I know God is a God of love, not of hate....How can I [put] down the fisherman when I've been fishing all my life?"[152]

In recognition of his contributions to music history, Richard was presented with the American Music Award's distinguished Award of Merit in 1997; and was inducted into the NAACP Image Awards' Hall of Fame. That same year, I met Richard on the set filming my movie, "Why Do Fools Fall In Love." He was as funny and fabulously entertaining as ever in his rendition of Keep A'Knockin'.

By 1998, the 66 year old icon was still touring extensively and flashing the energy and personality that his audiences loved. When asked how he felt at one point along the way, he broke out into that gorgeous, iconic Little Richard grin and quipped, "I'm still beautiful. I'm not conceited. I'm convinced!"[153]

Johnny Carson asked Richard on the Tonight Show, what he attributed his success to. Richard responded with characteristic wit...

"...Honey, I could scream like a white woman!"

After an appeal to the audience to live righteously, Little Richard sang spirituals, I Saw the Light, country songs Jambalaya, and even The Itsy Bitsy Spider. He

organized a singalong to *Tutti Frutti*, correcting the audience's attempts at *"A wop-bop-a-loo-mop, a lop-bam-
boom!"* as he shouted, "Don't mess up my song—that
song took me out of the kitchen!" He made it clear that
the last two syllables were "bam-boom," not "Pat Boone"
whose cover of *Tutti Frutti* rose higher than Richard's on
the Billboard charts back in the day. It was vintage Little
Richard.

Eventually, regarding his roles as both minister and
legendary Rock & Roll star, Richard had this to say:

Let me just say
this first, the work
that I am doing is
my job. I have to
eat, pay my rent,
pay my bills and
make a living like
everybody   else.
After seeing what
has happened to
certain ministers, I don't want to ever use the ministry
purely for financial reasons. Music and acting is my job.
That doesn't mean that I don't love God, I am still a
messenger for him as Little Richard.[154]

Then he repeated his famous 1979 statement made as
the Reverend Penniman at a revival in California:

*"If God can save an old homosexual like me, he
can save anybody."*

Epilogue

LEGACY

"Look anywhere...I am the only one left. I am the beautiful Little Richard from way down in Macon, Georgia. You know, Otis Redding is from there. And James Brown's from there, Wayne Cochran's from there. I was the best lookin' one so I left first. Prettiest thing in the kitchen, yes, sir! I want you to know I am the bronze Liberace! Shut up! Shut up!" [155]

Little Richard

Nineteen

Still Singin' an' Screamin' like a White Woman

L ittle Richard has reportedly been living the last several years in a penthouse suite at the Hilton hotel in downtown Nashville—even though the Hilton will not confirm nor deny that they have a guest there named Richard Penniman.

For 40 years Richard had oscillated between the pulpit and the stage but now he seemed to have found God and was comfortable being a "non-practicing" homosexual.

In 2000, a television biopic was made on Little Richard's life. It was not terribly truthful about his sexual preference—but Richard was an Executive Producer and the actor, Leon who portrayed him, was excellent.

Three years later, Richard was inducted into the Songwriters Hall of Fame, and his artistry has been unmatched in the seven decades since his emergence with *Tutti Frutti* which *Mojo magazine* declared as "The sound of the birth of Rock & Roll" in 2007.

But Richard's failing health in recent years has been well documented and he doesn't travel much anymore. Later in '07, he was having problems walking due to sciatica in his left leg. Two years later, Richard entered a hospital to have hip replacement surgery. The operation left him confined to a wheelchair or a cane for mobility. In a rare public appearance he admitted his hip surgery went horribly awry:

> I came to Nashville to see my sister. I bought a home for me and her here in the hills. And I went in for surgery on my hip. I was walking on my way in, but I couldn't walk out. The hip surgery was really bad for me. I haven't walked since. I'm in pain twenty-four hours a day. I have never seen nothing like it.[156]

Little Richard's *Tutti Frutti* was included in the National Recording Registry of the Library of Congress in 2010, which stated that his "unique vocalizing over the irresistible beat announced a new era in music."

Following this, despite the pain he was still in, Little Richard sang for President Barack Obama and First Lady Michelle Obama at the White House in 2011. It was the second time he had sung for a sitting United States President and a performance for which he was so prideful—for this President and First Lady were of African descent and he had lived long enough to see that history made.

Troubled by sciatica and his degenerating hip, Richard was performing sparingly and not always able to play up at his usual standards.

In June 2012, he had to stop a show telling the crowd, "Jesus, please help me, I can't hardly breathe. It's horrible." He recovered adequately enough to headline at the Orleans Hotel in Las Vegas during the Viva Las Vegas Rockabilly Weekend in March 2013. This would be his last concert performance before he officially retired. A year later, the legendary recording artist admitted that he was hanging it up and would not be performing again.

I am done, in a sense, because I don't feel like doing anything right now." He told the magazine adding, "I think my legacy should be that when I started in showbusiness there wasn't no such thing as rock 'n' roll. When I started with *Tutti Frutti*, that's when rock really started rocking."[157]

By 2015, people tried to get in touch with Little Richard for interviews, but he refused. He was in too much pain far too often. He told one writer:

People have been calling me from all over the world," he said. "But I haven't been doing any interviews, I've been refusing all of them. ...I'll be

eighty-three on December 5th [2015]. The Lord
has blessed me to still be alive.[158]

There was a story that once, in Nashville, a local
country singer happened to see Little Richard in his
black stretch chauffeur driven Cadillac Escalade and
shouted out Richard's name. Richard rolled down the
window and said, "God bless you," and handed him a
book of prayers.

That was around eleven in the morning when
Richard's Escalade rolled down Broadway and
turned onto Second Avenue to the Wildhorse Saloon in downtown Nashville.

That morning the city was open for early-bird
tourists, and there were cover bands playing Hank
and Elvis and Jerry Lee for them.

Richard's entourage—four men dressed in suits and
Secret Service shades—quickly lifted Richard out of
the passenger seat into his wheelchair and onto the
red carpet. He was being honored at a luncheon given
by the National Museum of African American Music. It
was called the Rhapsody & Rhythm Award for his pivotal
role in the formation of popular music genres and in
helping to shatter the color line on the music charts
changing American culture forever.

Wearing a paisley jacket adorned with a psychedelic
floral pattern over a polka-dot button-up shirt, a pompadour hairpiece, rhinestone boots, and gold sunglasses which he never removed. He looked like a man

in his 80s and was frail. He was also grumpy when he first arrived because the red carpet posed a problem. He did not want to be photographed in a wheelchair. "I really don't want anyone seeing me like this," he said.

But by the time he received his award, he was in a much better mood. The Architect of Rock & Roll, who at the time, had just entered his seventh decade in show-business, joked: "I'm over 80 years old, and I'm still singin' an' screamin' like a white woman."

Then he told stories about the old days in Nashville, playing gigs as a teenager at the New Era Club, sleeping at the YMCA because the white hotels wouldn't allow him to stay. He told members of the audience, "Y'all keep me in your prayers." He also told the Wildhorse audience:

> I just want y'all also to know that Jesus is coming soon. I'm serious. He's been talking to me and I just want you to know that and remember that something is fixing to happen in this old world. Get closer to God. All of you. Black people and white people. White people, you get closer too. He made you too. Everybody, get closer.[159]

Richard had said something similar two years earlier in a Rolling Stone magazine interview at a Recording Academy fundraiser in Atlanta, 2013. It may actually be his last interview for a publication. In it he said:

God talked to me the other night. He said He's getting ready to come. The world's getting ready to end...and He's coming, wrapped in flames of fire with a rainbow around his throne." [When someone in the audience laughed, Richard said]: "When I talk to you about God, I'm not playing.[160]

That evening Richard had been chatting with singer and songwriter CeeLo Green who told Richard he wanted to wear something fabulous, to make sure Richard didn't miss him. CeeLo was referring to his floor-length canary yellow kaftan when he and Richard were comparing wardrobe notes.

But Richard revealed to CeeLo, and later to the audience, a health crisis he'd recently experienced:

The other night, I didn't know I was having a heart attack. ...I was coughing, and my right arm was aching. I told my son, 'Make the room as cold as ice.' So he turned the air conditioning on, and I took a baby aspirin. The doctor told me that saved my life. Jesus had something for me. He brought me through."[161]

He told Jet magazine, *"God has never been far. ...I may stumble, but I didn't crumble, because He was there when I fumbled."*[162]

Now, having happily given his life over to God for the last time, Richard stopped all his indecisiveness regarding his love for the Rock of Ages. In his

interview with Three Angels Broadcasting Network
in September 2017, he said:

> God made men, men and he made women, women.
> Regardless of whatever you are, he loves you. You just
> have to say, Lord, take me as I am. I'm a sinner. We
> all have sinned and come short of the glory of God.[163]
> ...[Y]ou ain't tried anything until you've tried Jesus.
> He will show you the way because He is the Way. He
> will give you serenity and peace in this world and eter-
> nal life in the world to come. Make up your mind to
> give everything to Jesus. We ain't got long before
> we're going home."[164]

> ...I don't want to sing rock and roll no more. I want
> to be holy like Jesus."[165]

Yet, for many of us who love and revere Little Richard,
his music is holy too. It is the Gospel of memory. One as
prescient as that innocent, carefree time we return to
when we hear a particular tune of his, and reminisce on
where we were, what radio station we heard him on, who
we were dancing with, or what concert we saw him in.

For me it's hearing *Tutti Fruitti* and finding myself
hurled back to the hallway of my family's old Chicago
apartment dancing and singing, *"Awopaboppaloo-*
bopalopabingbang" not knowing the correct lyrics, but
loving the time I was having enjoying the record.
It makes me smile even now.

Writer Robert Chalmers who wrote an extensive interview piece for British GQ magazine stated it beautifully:

> Richard is, without question, the boldest and most in-
> fluential of the founding fathers of rock 'n' roll; one of
> the few genuine originals in an industry populated by
> performers whose appetite for fame greatly exceeds
> their talent."[166]

Even Ian Fraser "Lemmy" Kilmister of Motörhead has
weighed in:

> *Little Richard was always my main man. How*
> *hard must it have been for him: gay, black and*
> *singing in the South? But his records are a joy-*
> *ous good time from beginning to end.*[167]

But R&B pioneer Johnny Otis stated it best:

Little Richard is twice as valid artistically and important historically as Elvis Presley, the Beatles, and the Rolling Stones put together.[168]

Early in 2017, Richard's former girlfriend, Lee Angel travelled to Nashville to be with Richard.

I held him," she says. "It was just like it was in the old days," she told writer Jonny Whitehead, "He would never let me wear any clothes in bed, even though I had all these beautiful nightdresses. I held him close, while he went peacefully to sleep. It was as though we had travelled back in time 50 years.[169]

When asked in what way would she say Richard had been most misunderstood, Angel answered,

People will never know how generous he is, how many funerals he has paid for; how many people he has helped; how much rent he has paid for others. He is such a caring person. Such a giving person.[170]

Early in 2019, a resident of Macon, Georgia, Maggie Gonzalez, began a campaign proposing that a statue of Little Richard be erected in downtown Macon to take the place of a Confederate memorial currently occupying the space. Georgia law forbids tearing down Confederate statues. But they can be relocated. Gonzalez proposed that the Confederate statue be moved to Rose Hill

Cemetery in favor of Little Richard's statue as Macon's iconic son.

On October 23, 2019, at the Governor's Residence in Nashville, Tennessee, Little Richard received the Distinguished Artist Award at the Tennessee Governor's Arts Awards, the highest honor the state gives to artists. His appearance marked seventy-two years after he made his first appearance on the concert stage opening for Sister Rosetta Tharpe.

Little Richard is a survivor, and I love the comment he gave the Washington Post and Grunge magazine best:

> "I realized Rock 'n' Roll is my job and my belief is my belief. They're two separate things. I love what I'm doing and I put everything into it. Rock & Roll is something I created. It's all I know how to do; I don't know how to do anything else. I'm not a minister, and I'm not what you call a gospel singer, even though I've made some gospel records. I'm just an old country rock and roll singer from Macon, Georgia."[171] [172]

So rest easy Richard. No need to wonder if it's God's music or the Devil's. As Mavis Staples said: "It's *all* God's music...

...the Devil ain't got any."

Little Richard (center) surrounded by from L to R, Paul, Ringo, George and John of The Beatles, in 1963

Acknowledgements

A ll praise to God the father. Without him I would be lost. I also must thank from the bottom of my heart my dear friend and almost a life coach, Reuben Cannon who was the one to say, "You can do this."

Then, there is my crew at the Malibu Press. A huge thank you must go to Leigh Kirkwell, the executive editor who is exhaustively supportive and designed the book fabulously; Denise Gillman who read the first draft and gave fantastic notes. My editor, Belinda Curry who went through reams of material to help me streamline. Your critical analysis was invaluable, and I am nothing without you.

Along the way, there are angels who keep you going when you feel at odds or unsure. My enduring thanks to Erik Washington, who accepted every phone call and text, and is always there rain or shine with a positive word and a glass of wine; eternal thanks to Dr. Sharon D. Johnson who never tired of my questions, and Karen Jordan, my sushi running buddy, who made sure I'd eat by bringing down plates of food so graciously cooked by her mother Geraldine Jordan; Stanley Bennett Clay, who kept urging me on; and Marion Ramsey—who always makes me laugh. Another big shout out must go to my UK peeps, Ira Trattner, who always makes London fabulous; and Candace Turrey, my new partner-in-film crimes

Finally, there is "Little Richard" Penniman himself. Thank you for the music which has continued through the ages—and the life so filled with extraordinary adventures. Feel better, my lion of a talent. Know that without you most of the stars we have today would not exist. You are the shoulders upon whom Rock & Roll enduringly stands.

Discography

ALBUMS

Here's Little Richard (1957)
Little Richard (1958)
The Fabulous Little Richard (1958)
Pray Along with Little Richard (1960)
Pray Along with Little Richard (Vol 2) (1960)
The King of the Gospel Singers (1962)
Little Richard Is Back (And There's A Whole Lotta Shakin' Goin' On!) (1964)
Little Richard's Greatest Hits (1965)
The Incredible Little Richard Sings His Greatest Hits – Live! (1967)
The Wild and Frantic Little Richard (1967)
The Explosive Little Richard (1967)
Little Richard's Greatest Hits: Recorded Live! (1967)
The Rill Thing (1970)
Mr. Big (1971)
The King of Rock and Roll (1971)
Friends from the Beginning – Little Richard and Jimi Hendrix (1972)
Southern Child (1972) unreleased
Second Coming (1972)
Right Now! (1974)

Talkin' 'bout Soul (1974)
Little Richard Live (1976)
God's Beautiful City (1979)
Lifetime Friend (1986)
Shake It All About (1992)
Little Richard Meets Masayoshi Takanaka (1992)

SINGLES

Date, Side /Title, Label, Chart Position
US/UK, Album

Nov. 1951	A "Taxi Blues" RCA Victor
	B "Every Hour"
Feb. 1952	A "Get Rich Quick" RCA Victor
	B "Thinkin' 'Bout My Mother"
May 1952	A "Ain't Nothin' Happenin'" RCA Victor
	B "Why Did You Leave Me"
Nov 1952	A "Please Have Mercy" RCA Victor
	B "I Brought It All on Myself"
June, 1953	A "Ain't That Good News" (credit: Duces of Rhythm and Tempo Toppers, lead Little Richard) Peacock Records
	B "Fool at the Wheel" (credit: Duces of Rhythm and Tempo Toppers, lead Little Richard)
Mar, 1954	A "Always" (credit: Tempo Toppers feat. Little Richard) Peacock
	B "Rice, Red Beans and Turnip Greens" (Tempo Toppers feat. Little Richard)
Oct, 1955	A "Tutti Frutti" Specialty Records 1 (US) 2 (UK) *Here's Little Richard*

B "I'm Just a Lonely Guy" *The Fabulous Little Richard*

Mar, 1956   A "Long Tall Sally"   Specialty Records   1 (US) *Here's Little Richard*

B "Slippin' and Slidin'" 2 (US)

Apr, 1956   A *"Little Richard's Boogie"* (with Johnny Otis' band) Peacock 5-1658

B *"Directly from My Heart to You"* re-recorded for *The Fabulous Little Richard*

Jun, 1956   A "Rip It Up" Specialty   27 (US) 1 (UK) *Here's Little Richard*

B "Ready Teddy"   44 (US) 8 (UK)

Oct, 1956   A "Heeby-Jeebies" 7(US) *Little Richard*

B "She's Got It" 9 (US) 15 (UK) *Here's Little Richard*

Dec, 1956   A "The Girl Can't Help It" Specialty 7 (US) 9 (UK) *Little Richard*

B "All Around the World"   13 US)

Feb, 1957   A "Lucille"   Specialty   1 (US) 10 (UK)

B "Send Me Some Lovin'" 54 (US) 3 (UK)

Jun, 1957   A "Jenny, Jenny" Specialty 2 (US) 11(UK) *Here's Little Richard*

B "Miss Ann"   56 (US) 6 (UK)

Jul, 1957   A "Maybe I'm Right" (with Johnny Otis' band) Peacock, re-recorded for *The Fabulous Little Richard*

B "I Love My Baby" (w/Johnny Otis band)

Aug, 1957   A "Keep A-Knockin'" Specialty 2 (US) 21 (UK) *Little Richard*

B "Can't Believe You Wanna Leave" *Here's Little Richard*

Jan, 1958	A "Good Golly, Miss Molly" Specialty 4 (US) 8 (UK) *Little Richard*
	B "Hey-Hey-Hey-Hey!"
May, 1958	A "Ooh! My Soul" Specialty 15 (US) 22 (UK)
	B "True Fine Mama" 68 *Here's Little Richard*
July, 1958	A "Baby Face" Specialty 12 (US), 2 (UK) *Little Richard*
	B "I'll Never Let You Go (Boo Hoo Hoo Hoo)"
Nov, 1958	A "She Knows How to Rock" Specialty *The Fabulous Little Richard*
	B "Early One Morning"
Mar, 1959	A "By the Light of the Silvery Moon" Specialty 17 (US) *Little Richard*
	B "Wonderin'" *The Fabulous Little Richard*
Apr, 1959	A "Kansas City" Specialty 95 (US), 26 (UK) *The Fabulous Little Richard*
	B "Lonesome and Blue"
Jun, 1959	A "Shake a Hand" Specialty
	B "All Night Long"
Aug, 1959	A "Whole Lotta Shakin'" Specialty
	B "Maybe I'm Right"
Aug, 1959	A "I Got It" (alternate version of "She's Got It") Specialty N/A
	B "Baby" *Here's Little Richard*
Sep, 1959	A "Save Me Lord" End Records *Pray Along with Little Richard (Vol 2)*
	B "Troubles of the World"
Sep, 1959	A "Milky White Way" End *Pray Along*

with Little Richard (Vol 1)
B "I've Just Come from the Mountain"

1959   A "Directly from My Heart to You" Specialty *The Fabulous Little Richard*
B "The Most I Can Offer"

Sep, 1961   A "He's Not Just a Soldier" Mercury
The King of the Gospel Singers
B "Joy Joy Joy"

Jan, 1962   A "Ride On, King Jesus" Mercury
B "Do You Care"

May, 1962   A "He Got What He Wanted (But He Lost What He Had)" Mercury 38 (US)
B "Why Don't You Change Your Ways"

Dec, 1962   A "I'm in Love Again" (credit: The World Famous Upsetters) Little Star
B "Every Night About This Time" (credit: The World Famous Upsetters)

Feb, 1963   A "Crying in the Chapel" Atlantic
B "Hole in the Wall"

May, 1963   A "Traveling Shoes" Atlantic
B "It Is No Secret"

Oct, 1963   A "Milky White Way" Coral Records *Pray Along with Little Richard (Vol 1)*
B "Need Him"

1963   A "Valley of Tears" (credit: The World Famous Upsetters) Little Star
B "Freedom Ride" (credit: The World Famous Upsetters)

Apr, 1964   A "Bama Lama Bama Loo" Specialty 82 (US), 20 (UK)
B "Annie Is Back"

Aug, 1964   A "Whole Lotta Shakin' Goin' On" Vee Jay

Little Richard is Back (And There's a Whole Lotta Shakin' Goin' On!)

B "Goodnight Irene"

Nov, 1964   A "Blueberry Hill" Vee Jay

B "Cherry Red"

Feb, 1965   A "Cross Over" Vee Jay N/A

B "It Ain't Whatcha Do (It's the Way How You Do It)"

Jun, 1965   A "Without Love" Vee Jay

B "Dance What You Wanna"

Oct, 1965   A "I Don't Know What You've Got But It's Got Me – Part I" Vee Jay, 12 (US)

B "I Don't Know What You've Got But It's Got Me – Part II" 12 (US)

Jan, 1966   A "Holy Mackerel" Modern   Records, *The Wild and Frantic Little Richard*

B "Baby, Don't You Want a Man Like Me"

Feb, 1966   A "Do You Feel It (Part 1)" Modern Records *The Incredible Little Richard Sings His Greatest Hits – Live!* Over dubbed w/additional audience sounds

B "Do You Feel It (Part 2)"

Jun, 1966   A "Poor Dog (Who Can't Wag His Own Tail)" Okeh 41 (US) *The Explosive Lit tle Richard*

B "Well"

Jul, 1966   A "Direct from My Heart" Modern Records, *The Wild and Frantic Little Rich ard*

B "I'm Back"

Nov, 1966   A "I Need Love", Okeh *The Explosive Little Richard*

	B "The Commandments of Love"
Jan, 1967	A "I Don't Want to Discuss It" Okeh
	B "Hurry Sundown"
Feb, 1967	A "Get Down with It" CBS (UK)
	B "Rosemary"
Mar, 1967	A "Don't Deceive Me" Okeh *The Explosive Little Richard*
	B "Never Gonna Let You Go"
Jun, 1967	A "A Little Bit of Something (Beats a Whole Lot of Nothing)" Okeh
	B "Money" *The Explosive Little Richard*
1967	A "Bring It Back Home to Me" Modern Records, *The Incredible Little Richard Sings His Greatest Hits – Live!*
	B "Slippin' and Slidin'"
Nov, 1967	A "Baby What You Want Me to Do (Part 1)" Modern Records *The Wild and Frantic Little Richard*
	B "Baby What You Want Me to Do (Pt 2)"
Dec, 1967	A "Try Some of Mine", Brunswick
	B "She's Together"
Jun, 1968	A "Baby, Don't You Tear My Clothes" Brunswick
	B "Stingy Jenny"
Sep, 1968	A "Soul Train" Brunswick
	B "Can I Count on You"
Mar, 1969	A "Whole Lotta Shakin' Goin' On", Okeh *Little Richard's Greatest Hits: Live!*
	B "Lucille"
Apr, 1970	A "Bama Lama Bama Loo" (alt take) Specialty
	B "Keep A-Knockin'" (original version)

Little Richard

Apr, 1970	A	"Freedom Blues" Reprise 47 (US), 28 (UK) *The Rill Thing*
	B	"Dew Drop Inn"
Aug, 1970	A	"Greenwood, Mississippi", Reprise
	B	"I Saw Her Standing There"
Nov, 1970	A	"Poor Boy Paul" Specialty
	B	"Wonderin'", *The Fabulous Little Richard*
Mar, 1971	A	"Shake a Hand (If You Can)" (new version) Reprise
	B	"Somebody Saw You", *The Rill Thing*
Oct, 1971	A	"Green Power" Reprise *The King of Rock and Roll*
	B	"Dancing in the Street"
Nov, 1972	A	"Mockingbird Sally", Reprise, *The Second Coming*
	B	"Nuki Suki"
1972	A	"Goodnight Irene", (reissue; with Jimi Hendrix), ALA *Friends from the Beginning*
	B	"Why Don't You Love Me"
May, 1973	A	"Good Golly Miss Molly" (live). Bell, *Let the Good Times Roll (soundtrack)*
	B	"Lucille" (live)
Jun, 1973	A	"In the Middle of the Night" Greene Mountain, 71 (US)
	B	"Where Do I Find a Place to Sleep Now"
1973	A	"In the Name" Kent, *Right Now!*
	B	"Don't You Know"
Dec, 1975	A	"Call My Name" Manticore, 106 (US)
	B	"Steal Miss Liza"

1975	A "Try to Help Your Brother", Main stream
	B "Funk Proof"
1977	A1 "Good Golly Miss Molly", Creole, 37 (US), *Little Richard Live*
	A2 "Rip It Up"
	B "By the Light of the Silvery Moon"
Sep, 1983	A "Chicken Little Baby", Specialty, *The Fabulous Little Richard*
	B "Oh Why", *Here's Little Richard*
Circa, 1984	A "All Around the World", Specialty *Little Richard*
	B "Heeby-Jeebies-Love"
1986	A "Great Gosh A'Mighty! (It's a Matter of Time)" MCA, 42 (US), 62 (UK), *Down and Out in Beverly Hills (sound track)*
1986	A "Operator", WEA, 67 (US) *Lifetime Friend*
	B "Big House Reunion"
Jan, 1987	A "Somebody's Comin'" WEA, 93 (US)
	B "One Ray of Sunshine"
1988	A "Twins" (from the original film *Twins* (with Philip Bailey, 3:18), WTG, 82 (US)
	B "Twins" (from the original motion pic ture "Twins") (with Philip Bailey, 3:57) 82 (US)

LIVE ALBUMS

The Incredible Little Richard Sings His Greatest Hits – Live!, Released: 1966 or 1967 Label: Modern Format: stereo LP

Little Richard's Greatest Hits: Recorded Live!, Released: July 1967, Label: Okeh, Format: stereo LP, 184, 28

COMPILATION ALBUMS

1960: *Little Richard Sings: Clap Your Hands* (Spinorama M119)

1963: *Sings Spirituals*

1963: *His Biggest Hits* (Specialty SP-2111)

1964: *Sings the Gospel*

1966-67: *The Wild and Frantic Little Richard*

1967: *Rock N Roll Forever*

1968: *Little Richard's Grooviest 17 Original Hits* (Specialty)

1968: *Forever Yours* (Roulette)

1969: *Good Golly Miss Molly*

1969: *Little Richard*

1970: *Rock Hard Rock Heavy*

1970: *Little Richard*

1970: *Well Alright!*

1971: *Mr. Big*

1972: *The Original*

1972: *Friends from the Beginning – Little Richard and Jimi Hendrix*

1972: *Super Hits* (Trip; gatefold)

1973: *Rip It Up*

1974: *Recorded Live*

1974: *Talkin' 'bout Soul*

1975: *Keep a Knockin'*

1976: *Sings*

1977: *Now*

1977: *22 Original Hits* (Warwick)

1983: *20 Greatest Hits* (Lotus)

1984: *Little Richard's Greatest* (Kent)

1985: *18 Greatest Hits* (Rhino)

1988: *Lucille*

1990: *The Essential Little Richard*

1991: *The Georgia Peach*

1996: *Shag on Down by the Union Hall Featuring Shea Sandlin & Richard "The Sex" Hounsome*

1996: *Little Richard's Grand Slam Hits* (DIMI Music Group)

2006: *Here Comes Little Richard/Little Richard*

2008: *The Very Best of Little Richard*

2016: *California (I'm Comin')*

LABEL OVERVIEWS

1989: *The Specialty Sessions* (Ace, UK, 6CD; truncated 3CD version released in US on Specialty)

1996: *The Second Coming* (Charly; also released as *Dancin' All Around the World – The Complete Vee-Jay Recordings*; all previously released, missing alternate take of "I Don't Know What You've Got", and unreleased material)

2004: *Get Down With It: The Complete Okeh Sessions* (all studio; no live; Columbia)

2005: *King Of Rock and Roll: The Complete Reprise Sessions* (Rhino Handmade)

2005: *Get Rich Quick – Birth of a Legend, 1951–1954* (RCA, Peacock, Republic; Rev-Ola)

2015: *Directly from My Heart: The Best of the Specialty & Vee-Jay Years* (Concord Music Group)

GUEST APPEARANCES / DUETS

Year, Song, Album

1970, "Miss Ann", *To Bonnie from Delaney* (Delaney & Bonnie And Friends album)

1970, "Bludgeon of a Bluecoat – The Man", Unreleased track with Joey Covington of Jefferson Airplane

1971, "Money Is" and "Do It", Dollars (Quincy Jones album)

1972, "He's Not Just a Soldier", Mylon LeFevre album

1975, "Take It Like A Man", *Head On*

1985, "Great Gosh A'Mighty", *Down and Out in Beverly Hills* Soundtrack

1987, "Happy Endings", *The Telephone* Soundtrack

1988, "Rock Island Line", *Folkways: A Vision Shared – A Tribute to Woody Guthrie & Leadbelly*

1988, "Twins", *Twins* Soundtrack

1989, "When Love Comes to Town" (Live From The Kingdom Mix), 12" extended mix of the U2/B.B. King song

1990, "Elvis Is Dead", *Time's Up*

1990, "You Really Got Me Now", *Young Guns* film soundtrack

1991, "Voices That Care",

1991, "Itsy Bitsy Spider", *Disney For Our Children*

1991, "The Power", *Duets*

1994, "Somethin' Else", *Rhythm, Country and Blues*

1996, "Everybody's Got A Game", *Definition of Soul*

1997, "Hold On To What You've Got", *Soul-Gasm*

1999, "Keep A'Knockin'", *Why Do Fools Fall In Love* Soundtrack

2002, "Get Rhythm", *Kindred Spirits: A Tribute to the Songs of Johnny Cash*

2006, "I Saw Her Standing There", *Last Man Standing*

2008, "I Ain't Never", *The Imus Ranch Record*

2011, "He Ain't Never Done Me Nothing But Good", Dottie Rambo tribute album (unreleased)

2012, "But I Try", Released in 2012 on Joe Walsh's CD *Analog Man*

Filmography

The Girl Can't Help It (1956), lip-syncing the title number "Ready Teddy" and "She's Got It"

Don't Knock the Rock (1956), lip-syncing "Long Tall Sally" and "Tutti Frutti"

Mister Rock and Roll (1957), lip-syncing "Lucille" and "Keep A-Knockin'", on original prints

Catalina Caper (aka *Never Steal Anything Wet*, 1967), Richard lip-syncs an original tune, "Scuba Party", still unreleased on record by 2019.

Little Richard: Live at the Toronto Peace Festival (1969) – released on DVD in 2009 by Shout! Factory

The London Rock & Roll Show (1973), performing "Lucille", "Rip It Up", "Good Golly Miss Molly", "Tutti Frutti", "I Believe", and "Jenny Jenny"

Jimi Hendrix (1973)

Let the Good Times Roll (1973) featured performances and behind-the-scenes candid footage of Little Richard, Chuck Berry, Bo Diddley, Fats Domino, Bill Haley, the Five Satins, the Shirelles, Chubby Checker, and Danny and the Juniors.

Down and Out in Beverly Hills (1986), co-starred as Orvis Goodnight and performed the production number, "Great Gosh A-Mighty"

Miami Vice, (1985)*"Out Where the Buses Don't Run"*, costarred as Rev. Marvelle Quinn.

Hail! Hail! Rock 'n' Roll TV Documentary (1987)

Goddess of Love Made For TV Movie (1988)

Purple People Eater (1988)

Scenes from the Class Struggle in Beverly Hills (1989)

Bill & Ted's Excellent Adventures (1990) (voice)

Mother Goose Rock 'n' Rhyme (1990)

Columbo - S10E3 "Columbo and the Murder of a Rock Star" (1991) (Cameo)

The Naked Truth (1992)

Sunset Heat (aka *Midnight Heat*) (1992)

James Brown: The Man, The Message, The Music TV Documentary (1992)

Martin as the exterminator (1992)

The Pickle (1993)

Last Action Hero (1993)

Full House (1994) (Cameo) - Episode: Too Little Richard Too Late

Baywatch (1995) as Maurice in Episode: The Runaways

The Drew Carey Show (1997) (cameo) - Episode: Drewstock

Why Do Fools Fall in Love (1998) as himself. Performed "Keep A'Knockin'

Mystery Alaska (1999)

The Trumpet of the Swan (2001) (voice)

The Simpsons (2002) (voice)

SOURCES

Age, The. *Negro Singer Has Colorful Debut*, (newspaper), Sydney, Australia, October 9, 1957

Alexander, Phil. *When Jimi Hendrix Met Little Richard, Brother Leon Hendrix Remembers the Future Guitar Legend's Fateful First Encounter with Rock 'n' Roll's Georgia Peach*. Mojo Magazine, December 13, 2013

Bell, Robin. *The History of British Rock 'n' Roll: The Beat Boom 1963-1966*. Robin Bell, 2016

Blackwell, Roger, and Tina Stephans. *Brands That Rock: What Business Leaders Can Learn from the World of Rock and Roll*. Hoboken. John Wiley & Sons, 2004.

Brown, Tony *Jimi Hendrix: "Talking."* London. Omnibus Press, 2003, pgs. 31–34.

Chalmers, Robert. *Legend: Little Richard*. British GQ Magazine, March 29, 2012

Charles River Editors. *American Legends: The Life of Little Richard*. CreateSpace Independent Publishing Platform, 2015

Coleman, Rick. *Blue Monday: Fats Domino and the Lost Dawn of Rock 'n' Roll*. Boston. Da Capo Press, 2007

Collier, Aldore. *"Little Richard Tells Us How He Got What He Wanted But Lost What He Had. Jet Magazine.* Vol. 67 no. 12. November 26, 1984

Cross, Charles R. *Room Full of Mirrors, A Biography of Jimi Hendrix.* New York. Hyperion, Hachette Books, 2005

Dalton, David. Rolling Stone Magazine, *Little Richard: Child of God, An Interview with the Legend of Rock and R&B,* May 28, 1970

DiCesare, Pat. Pat DiCesare Blog, *Good Golly, Little Richard! You Sure Influenced The Beatles!* http://www.concertpat.com/good-golly-little-richard-sure-influenced-beatles/ February 2015

Demaret, Kent. People Magazine; *The Temptations of Rock Behind Him, Little Richard Becomes a Bible Salesman,* January 08, 1979

Du Bois, W.E.B. *The Souls of Black Folks.* Mineola, NY. Dover Publications, 1994

Everett, Walter. *The Beatles as Musicians: The Quarry Men through Rubber Soul.* New York. Oxford University Press. 2001.

Frith, Simon. *The Sociology of Rock, (Communication and Society).* New York. Constable & Robinson Ltd., 1978

Garodkin, John. *Little Richard, King of Rock 'n' Roll.* Copenhagen. C. P. Wulff, 1975

Gilliland, John. *Big Rock Candy Mountain: Rock 'n' roll in the late fifties.* (audio).*Pop Chronicles.* University of North Texas Libraries. 1969.

Grimes, A.C. *The Untold Truth of Little Richard.* www.grunge.com/93930/untold-truth-little-richard/

Gulla, Bob. *Icons of R&B and Soul: An Encyclopedia of the Artists Who Revolutionized Rhythm.* 2008.

Guralnick, Peter. *Sweet Soul Music: Rhythm and Blues and the Southern Dream of Freedom.* New York. Back Bay Books, 1999.

———. *Dream Boogie: The Triumph of Sam Cooke.* New York. Back Bay Books, 2006

Hamilton, Anita. 50 Plus World, *Little Richard Is 84 – His Story and Songs.* December 6, 2016. https://50plusworld.com/little-richard-is-84-his-story-and-songs/

Hamilton, Jack. *Just Around Midnight: Rock and Roll and the Racial Imagination.* Cambridge. Harvard University press, 2016

Hamilton, Marybeth. *Sexual Politics and African-American Music; Or, Placing Little Richard in History. History Workshop Journal,* No. 46. Oxford University Press, 1998. Retrieved from http://www.jstor.org/stable/4289584

Hannusch, Jeff. *I Hear You Knockin': The Sound of New Orleans Rhythm and Blues.* Ville Platte, Louisiana. Swallow Publications, Inc. 1985

Harry, Bill. *The Paul McCartney Encyclopedia.* Virgin. 2002

Havers, Richard. *Revisiting The Rolling Stones' First Tour, September 29, 1963* Published on September

29, 2018 https://www.udiscovermusic.com/stories/rolling-stones-first-tour/

Henderson, David. *'Scuse Me While I Kiss the Sky: Jimi Hendrix: Voodoo Child.* New York. Simon & Schuster, 2008

Himes, Geoffrey, *It's Still Rock 'n' Roll for Little Richard.* Washington Post, May 28, 1999

Hinckley, David. *The Rolling Stones: Black & White Blues.* Nashville. Turner Publishing Inc. 1995.

Kamp, David. *The Oral History: The British Invasion.* Vanity Fair (magazine), November 2002.

Kemp, Mark. *Dixie Lullaby: A Story of Music, Race, and New Beginnings in a New South.* New York. Free Press. 2004

Kirby, David. *Little Richard The Birth of Rock 'n' Roll.* New York. Continuum Books, 2009

Krerowicz, Aaron. *The Influence of Little Richard on the Beatles.* https://www.aaronkrerowicz.com/beatles-blog/the-influence-of-little-richard-on-the-beatles March 14, 2014.

Lewisohn, Mark. *The Complete Beatles Chronicle.* Pyramid Books, (imprint of Octopus Publishing Group Limited) London, UK, 2006.

Luling, Todd Van. *11 Stories You Still Haven't Heard About The Beatles, Based On Their Earliest Interviews. The Huffington Post.* TheHuffingtonPost.com Sept 28, 2016. https://www.huffpost.com/entry/beatles-trivia_n_7572788

Mahon, Maureen. *Right to Rock: The Black Rock Coalition and the Cultural Politics of Race*. Duke University Press, 2004

Marshall, James "The Hound." *The Hound NYC. Billy Wright.* https://thehound-nyc.com/2009/06/15/billy-wright/ 6/15/09

Miles, Barry. *Paul McCartney: Many Years From Now*. New York. Henry Holt and Company, 1997

Miller, Zell. *They Heard Georgia Singing [Little Richard]*. Mercer University Press;1996

Mojo (magazine), Mojo4Music.com, June, 2007; No. 129

Murray, Charles Shaar. *Crosstown Traffic: Jimi Hendrix and the Rock 'n' Roll Revolution*. New York. St. Martin's Press, 1989

Newcastle Morning Herald newspaper, (Melbourne, Australia) 10/3/57

Norman, Philip. *Mick Jagger*. New York. Ecco Press, 2012

Noxon, Christopher. *Little Richard the Lionhearted*, Los Angeles Times February 20, 2000

Open Vault From WGBH. *Rock and Roll; Renegades; Interview with Dorothy LaBostrie*. Boston, MA: WGBH Media Library & Archives.

Oscala Star Banner, *Little Richard Files Suit To Claim Lost Royalties,* August 17, 1984

Oxford American Magazine. *Prayers For Richard*. Issue 91, Winter 2015, December 11, 2015

Powers, Ann. *Good Booty: Love and Sex, Black and White, Body and Soul in American Music.* New York. Dey Street Books, 2017

Ramsey, David. *Prayers for Richard.* Oxford American (magazine). December 11, 2015

Richards, Keith. *Life.* New York. Back Bay Books, 2011

Rhodes, Don. *Say It Loud!: The Life of James Brown, Soul Brother No. 1.* Guilford, Connecticut. Lyons Press, 2014

Roberts, David. *British Hit Singles & Albums* (19th ed.). London. Guinness World Records Limited, 2006. P. 324

Roby, Steven and Brad Schreiber. *Becoming Jimi Hendrix, From Southern Crossroads to Psychedelic London, The Untold Story of a Musical Genius.* Boston. Da Capo Press, 2010

Rock & Roll Hall of Fame, *Little Richard Biography*

Rolling Stone, *Little Richard Biography*

Sales, Soupy. *Soupy Sez: My Zany Life and Times.* New York. M. Evans and Company, Inc., 2003

Shadwick, Keith. *Jimi Hendrix Musician.* San Francisco. Backbeat Books, 2003

South Bank Show (UK). *Little Richard Interview,* March 1985

Three Angels Broadcasting Network. *"3ABN Today Live – Interview with "Little Richard"–* via YouTube. (September 6, 2017) and (October 19, 2017)

Unterberger, Richie. *Artist Biography, Little Richard*

Waldron, Clarence. *Life Story of Rock 'n' Roll Legend Little Richard Told in NBC Movie.* Jet Magazine, February 2000

Walker, Alice. *You Can't Keep a Good Woman Down* (Collection of Short Stories); *Nineteen Fifty-Five.* Boston. Houghton Mifflin Harcourt Publishing Company, 1982

Waters, John. *Role Models.* New York. Farrar, Straus and Giroux, 2010

White, Charles. *The Life and Times of Little Richard, The Quasar of Rock.* New York. Harmony Books, 1984

Whiteside, Jonny. *Lee Angel: The Muse Who Had A Front-Row Seat To Rock History.* LA Weekly, May 31, 2018

Wood, Ronnie. *The Ronnie Wood Show. Rolling Stones guitarist Ron Wood interviews Paul McCartney about touring with Little Richard in Hamburg, Germany, 1962.* Via YouTube. https://www.youtube.com/watch?v = HZxqyYQRV5U

Wooten, Kristi York. Rolling Stone Magazine, *Little Richard Tells Cee Lo About Recent Heart Attack 'Jesus Brought Me Through,' he says.* September 30, 2013.

Endnotes

[1] Song Facts https://www.songfacts.com/facts/little-richard
[2] Kirby, David. *Little Richard The Birth of Rock 'n' Roll*. New York. Continuum, 2009. Pg. 13
[3] Ewbank, Tim. *Rod Stewart: The New Biography*. Citadel Press, 2005.
[4] Doggett, Peter. *Teenage Wildlife*. *Mojo Classic*. January 2007
[5] Elton John quoted in Blackwell, 2004, pg. 65.
[6] Harry, Bill. *The Paul McCartney Encyclopedia*. Virgin. 2002
[7] Murray, Charles. *Crosstown Traffic: Jimi Hendrix and the Rock 'n' Roll Revolution*. St. Martin's Press. 1989
[8] Sanneh, Kelefa. *MUSIC; Rappers Who Definitely Know How to Rock*. The New York Times, December 3, 2000
[9] Caramanica, Jon. *Speakerboxxx/The Love Below*. Rolling Stone, September 24, 2003.
[10] *Bruno Mars: 99 Reasons Why He's the Biggest Pop Star in the World*—National Post.
[11] *Critic's Notebook: Bruno Mars in Ascension. New York Times*. October 6, 2010.
[12] Walker, Alice. You Can't Keep a Good Woman Down (Collection of Short Stories); *Nineteen Fifty-Five*, Boston. Houghton Mifflin Harcourt Publishing Company, 1982
[13] Murray, Charles Shaar. *Crosstown Traffic, Jimi Hendrix and the Post-War Rock 'n' Roll Revolution*. New York. St. Martin's Press, 1989
[14] Interview with Little Richard. Washington Post, 1999
[15] Rock & Roll Hall of Fame. *Beatles accept award Rock and Roll Hall of Fame inductions 1988*. January 28, 2010 – via YouTube.

[16] Quoted from: Three Angels Broadcasting *3ABN Today Live - Interview with "Little Richard"*– via *YouTube* Network *(September 6, 2017)*

[17] Chalmers, Robert. *Legend: Little Richard*. British GQ magazine, March 29, 2012

[18] White, Charles. *Life and Times of Little Richard, Quasar of Rock*.

[19] Southwest Georgia, Little Richard – www.southwest-ga.com/famous-people/little-richard.html

[20] Du Bois, W.E.B. *The Souls of Black Folks*. Mineola, NY. Dover Publications, 1994

[21] Baldwin, James. *The Fire Next Time*. New York. Vintage Books; Reissue ed., 1992

[22] Puterbaugh, Parke. Rolling Stone Magazine. *Little Richard: 'I Am the Architect of Rock & Roll' The Georgia Peach, the Living Flame, the Southern Child, the King of Rock & Roll: Little Richard is all of these, and he'll be the first to tell you so.* April 19, 1990.

[23] Himes, Geoffrey. The Washington Post. *It's Still Rock 'n' Roll for Little Richard*. May 28, 1999

[24] Demaret, Kent. People Magazine; *The Temptations of Rock Behind Him, Little Richard Becomes a Bible Salesman*, January 08, 1979

[25] Dalton, David. *Little Richard: Child of God: An Interview with the Legend of Rock and R&B;* Rolling Stone magazine, May 28, 1970

[26] Demaret, Kent. People Magazine; *The Temptations of Rock Behind Him, Little Richard Becomes a Bible Salesman*, January 08, 1979

[27] White, Charles. *Life and Times of Little Richard, Quasar of Rock*. pg. 25

[28] Marshall, James "The Hound" *The HoundNYC. Billy Wright.* https://thehoundnyc.com/2009/06/15/billy-wright/

[29] Rock & Roll Hall of Fame, *Little Richard Biography*

[30] Chalmers, Robert. *Legend: Little Richard*. British GQ magazine, March 29, 2012

[31] White, Charles. *Life and Times of Little Richard, Quasar of Rock*. pg. 17

[32] Ibid. pg. 20

[33] Ibid.

[34] Ibid.

[35] Ibid. pg. 21

[36] Waldron, Clarence. *Life Story of Rock 'n' Roll Legend Little Richard Told in NBC Movie.* Jet Magazine, February, 2000, pg. 65

[37] Hamilton, Anita. 50 Plus World *Little Richard Is 84 - His Story and Songs.*(December 6, 2016) https://50plusworld.com/little-richard-is-84-his-story-and-songs/

[38] Ibid.

[39] Ibid.

[40] Ibid. pg. 22

[41] White, Charles. *Life and Times of Little Richard, Quasar of Rock.* pg. 33

[42] Waters, John. *Role Models.* New York. Farrar, Straus and Giroux, 2010

[43] White, Charles. *Life and Times of Little Richard, Quasar of Rock.* pg. 33

[44] Chalmers, Robert. *Legend: Little Richard.* British GQ magazine, March 29, 2012

[45] Himes, Geoffrey. The Washington Post. *It's Still Rock 'n' Roll for Little Richard.* May 28, 1999

[46] Puterbaugh, Parke. Rolling Stone Magazine. *Little Richard: 'I Am the Architect of Rock & Roll' The Georgia Peach, the Living Flame, the Southern Child, the King of Rock & Roll: Little Richard is all of these, and he'll be the first to tell you so.* April 19, 1990.

[47] Ibid.

[48] Coleman, Rick. Liner notes, *Little Richard: The Specialty Sessions.* 1989

[49] Rhodes, Don. *Say It Loud!: The Life of James Brown, Soul Brother No. 1.* Guilford, Ct. Lyons Press, 2014

[50] Chalmers, Robert. *Legend: Little Richard.* British GQ magazine, March 29, 2012

[51] Ibid.

[52] Ibid.

[53] Mehr, Bob. Quoted from Mojo Magazine. *In The Beginning Was The Word.* June 2007

[54] White, Charles. *Life and Times of Little Richard, Quasar of Rock.* pg. 60

[55] Chalmers, Robert. *Legend: Little Richard.* British GQ magazine, March 29, 2012

[56] LaBostrie quote from: Hannusch, Jeff. *I Hear You Knockin': The Sound of New Orleans Rhythm and Blues*. Ville Platte, Louisiana. Swallow Publications, 1985, pgs. 220-222

[57] Open Vault From WGBH. *Rock and Roll; Renegades; Interview with Dorothy LaBostrie*. Boston, MA: WGBH Media Library & Archives.   Retrieved   from http://openvault.wgbh.org/catalog/V_CF6582 AFE3E0492587D87B54983733F7

[58] Guralnick, Peter. *Sweet Soul Music: Rhythm and Blues and the Southern Dream of Freedom*. New York. Back Bay Books, 1999.

[59] Mehr, Bob. Quoted from Mojo Magazine. *In The Beginning Was The Word*. June 2007

[60] Kirby, David. *Little Richard The Birth of Rock 'n' Roll*. New York. Continuum, 2009. Pgs. 117

[61] White, Charles. *Life and Times of Little Richard, Quasar of Rock*, pgs. 65-66

[62] Coleman, Rick. *Blue Monday: Fats Domino and the Lost Dawn of Rock 'n' Roll*. Boston. Da Capo Press, 2007

[63] Puterbaugh, Parke. Rolling Stone Magazine. *Little Richard: 'I Am the Architect of Rock & Roll' The Georgia Peach, the Living Flame, the Southern Child, the King of Rock & Roll: Little Richard is all of these, and he'll be the first to tell you so.* April 19, 1990.

[64] The Roanoke incident was drawn from *New York Times*, May 6, 1956, pg. 78; and the *Roanoke World News*, May 4, 1956, pg. B-12, and May 5, 1956

[65] White, Charles. *Life and Times of Little Richard, Quasar of Rock*, pg. 60-61

[66] Ibid. pg. 60

[67] Ibid. pg. 63

[68] Ibid.

[69] Kirby, David. *Little Richard The Birth of Rock 'n' Roll*. New York. Continuum, 2009. pgs. 69-70

[70] Bo Diddley quoted from *Chuck Berry: Hail! Hail! Rock and Roll*.

[71] White, Charles. *Life and Times of Little Richard, Quasar of Rock*, pg. 60

[72] Whiteside, Jonny. *Lee Angel: The Muse Who Had A Front-Row Seat To Rock History*. LA Weekly, May 31, 2018

[73] Ibid.

[74] White, Charles. *Life and Times of Little Richard, Quasar of Rock,* pgs. 72-73

[75] Chalmers, Robert. *Legend: Little Richard.* British GQ magazine, March 29, 2012

[76] Ibid.

[77] Topping, Ray, Art Rupe quoted from Liner notes on *Little Richard The Specialty Sessions,* 1989

[78] Quoted from, https://www.deejay.de/Various_Artists_Wild Streak Rock_N_Roll_Lp_VTRLP2039_Vinyl_175539 as found in FBI files.

[79] Newcastle Morning Herald newspaper, *Singer Dragged Over Footlights.* (Melbourne, Australia) 10/3/57

[80] The Age newspaper. *Negro Singer Has Colorful Debut, Sydney, Australia,* 1957 10/9

[81] White, Charles. *Life and Times of Little Richard, Quasar of Rock,* pgs. 91-92

[82] Ramsey, David. Oxford American magazine. *Prayers For Richard.* Issue 91, Winter 2015, December 11, 2015

[83] White, Charles. *Life and Times of Little Richard, Quasar of Rock,* pg. 94

[84] Ibid. pg. 98.

[85] Ibid. pgs. 98-99

[86] Ibid. 103

[87] Ibid. pg. 104

[88] Ibid. pg. 100

[89] Ibid. pg. 104

[90] Ibid. pg. 105

[91] Ibid. pg.106

[92] Richards, Keith. *Life.* New York. Back Bay Books, 2011

[93] Murray, Charles Shaar. *Crosstown Traffic.* New York. St. Martin's Press, 1989

[94] Guralnick, Peter. *Dream Boogie: The Triumph of Sam Cooke.* New York. Little Brown & Company, 2005

[95] Long Tall Sally lyrics by permission © Sony/ATV Music Publishing LLC. Songwriters: Entoris Johnson/Richard Penniman/Robert Blackwell.

[96] White, Charles. *Life and Times of Little Richard, Quasar of Rock,* pgs. 115-116

[97] Harry, Bill. *The Paul McCartney Encyclopedia*. Virgin. 2002, pg. 200

[98] DiCesare, Pat. Pat DiCesare Blog. *Good Golly, Little Richard! You Sure Influenced The Beatles!*

http://www.concertpat.com /good-golly-little-richard-sure-influenced-beatles/ February 17, 2015

[99] Miles, Miles, Barry. *Paul McCartney: Many Years From Now*. New York. Henry Holt and Company. pg. 201

[100] John Lennon Anthology (Booklet accompanying CDs), 1998

[101] Rolling Stones guitarist Ron Wood interviews Paul McCartney about Little Richard on his show *The Ronnie Wood Show*. Archived at https://www.youtube.com/watch?v= HZxqyYQRV5U

[102] Luling, Todd Van. *11 Stories You Still Haven't Heard About The Beatles, Based On Their Earliest Interviews. The Huffington Post*. TheHuffingtonPost.com Sept 28, 2016. https://www.huffpost.com/entry/beatles-trivia_n_7572788

[103] White, Charles. *Life and Times of Little Richard, Quasar of Rock, pg. 117*

[104] Havers, Richard. *Revisiting The Rolling Stones' First Tour*, September 29, 1963 Published on September 29, 2018 https://www.udiscovermusic.com/stories/rolling-stones-first-tour/

[105] JH. Disc (magazine) September 1963

[106] Leigh, Spencer, Spencer Leigh's On The *Beat, We Used To Have Good Times Together*. http://www. spencer-leigh.co.uk/2014/ 09/we-used-to-have-good-times-together

[107] Record Mirror, *Stones on Everlys and Diddley Tour*. October, 1962

[108] Richards, Keith. *Life*. New York. Back Bay Books, 2011

[109] Bell, Robin. The History of British Rock 'n' Roll: The Beat Boom 1963-1966. Robin Bell, 2016

[110] Record Mirror, *Stones on Everlys and Diddley Tour*. October, 1962

[111] Leigh, Spencer, Spencer Leigh's On The *Beat, We Used To Have Good Times Together*. http://www. spencer-leigh.co.uk/2014/ 09/we-used-to-have-good-times-together

[112] Richards, Keith. *Life*. New York. Back Bay Books, 2011. Pg. 134

113 White, Charles. *Life and Times of Little Richard, Quasar of Rock,* pg. 125

114 Rare and Unreleased, *Interview with Jimi Hendrix,* radio program, disc 1 track 3

115 *South Bank Show.*(UK) Interview with Little Richard. March, 1985

116 Alexander, Phil. *When Jimi Hendrix Met Little Richard, Brother Leon Hendrix remembers the future guitar legend's fateful first encounter with rock 'n' roll's Georgia Peach.* Mojo Magazine, December 13, 2013

117 Roby, Steven. *Becoming Jimi Hendrix.* Da Capo Press, pg. 119

118 Ibid. Pg. 101

119 Ibid.

120 Ibid. pg. 108

121 Ibid. Pg. 107

122 Puterbaugh, Parke. Rolling Stone (Magazine). *Little Richard: 'I Am the Architect of Rock & Roll' The Georgia Peach, the Living Flame, the Southern Child, the King of Rock & Roll: Little Richard is all of these, and he'll be the first to tell you so.* April 19, 1990.

123 Sales, Soupy. *Soupy Sez: My Zany Life and Times.* New York. M. Evans and Company, Inc., 2003

124 Roby, Steven. *Becoming Jimi Hendrix.* Da Capo Press, pg. 118

125 Ibid.

126 Kamp, David. *The Oral History: The British Invasion.* Vanity Fair (magazine), November 2002

127 Roby, Steven. *Becoming Jimi Hendrix.* Da Capo Press, pg. 118.

128 Ibid.

129 Cross, Charles R. *Room Full of Mirrors, A Biography of Jimi Hendrix.* New York. Hachette Books, 2005. Pg. 117

130 White, Charles. *Life and Times of Little Richard, Quasar of Rock,* pg. 132

131 Ibid.

132 Grimes, A. C. *The Untold Truth Of Little Richard.* Grunge Magazine.
https://www.grunge.com/93930/untold-truth-little-richard/

133 Cross, Charles R. *Room Full of Mirrors, A Biography of Jimi Hendrix.* New York. Hachette Books, 2005

134 Kirby, David. *Little Richard The Birth of Rock 'n' Roll.* New York. Continuum, 2009. pgs. 164-165

[135] Takiff, Jonathan. The Philadelphia Inquirer, *Joni Mitchell ran off-stage crying, Little Richard brought the house down: Why doesn't anyone remember the Atlantic City Pop Festival?* Updated: July 28, 2019

[136] Ibid.

[137] Unterberger, Richie. *Artist Biography, Little Richard*

[138] Whiteside, Jonny. *Lee Angel: The Muse Who Had A Front-Row Seat To Rock History.* LA Weekly, May 31, 2018

[139] Ibid.

[140] Little Richard on the *South Bank Show.*(UK) Interview with Little Richard, 1985

[141] Lee Angel on the *South Bank Show.*(UK) Interview with Little Richard, 1985

[142] Little Richard on the *South Bank Show.*(UK) Interview with Little Richard, 1985

[143] Chalmers, Robert. *Legend: Little Richard.* British GQ magazine, March 29, 2012

[144] Bumps Blackwell interview on the *South Bank Show.*(UK) Interview with Little Richard, 1985

[145] Noxon, Christopher. *Little Richard the Lionhearted.* Los Angeles Times, February 20, 2000

[146] Oscala Star Banner, *Little Richard Files Suit To Claim Lost Royalties,* August 17, 1984

[147] White, Charles. *Life and Times of Little Richard, Quasar of Rock.*

[148] Waters, John. *Role Models.* New York. Farrar, Straus and Giroux, 2010, Pg. 187

[149] Associated Press. *Little Richard Credits God for Crash Survival.* (found in the Los Angeles Times, October 26, 1985).

[150] Waters, John. *Role Models.* New York. Farrar, Straus and Giroux, 2010

[151] Ibid.

[152] Interview with Penthouse Magazine, 1995

[153] Rolling Stone magazine. *Little Richard Biography*

[154] White, Charles. *Life and Times of Little Richard, Quasar of Rock.*

[155] Dalton, David. Rolling Stone Magazine, *Little Richard: Child of God, An interview With the Legend of Rock and R&B,* May 28, 1970

[156] Ramsey, David. *Prayers for Richard*. Oxford American magazine. December 11, 2015

[157] Eames, Tom. Digital Spy *Little Richard Retires at 80*.

[158] Ibid.

[159] National Museum of African American Music. *My Music Matters: A Celebration of Legends Luncheon*. June 19, 2015.

[160] Wooten, Kristi York. Rolling Stone Magazine, *Little Richard Tells Cee Lo About Recent Heart Attack 'Jesus Brought Me Through,' He Says*. September 30, 2013

[161] Ibid.

[162] Waldron, Clarence. *Life Story of Rock 'n' Roll Legend Little Richard Told in NBC Movie*. Jet Magazine, February, 2000, pg. 65

[163] Three Angels Broadcasting Network *(September 6, 2017) 3ABN Today Live - Interview with "Little Richard"– via YouTube*

[164] Ibid.

[165] Ibid.

[166] Chalmers, Robert. *Legend: Little Richard*. British GQ magazine, March 29, 2012

[167] Simmons, Sylvie. *"Last night a record changed my life"*. Mojo magazine, No. 129. August 2004, pg. 30.

[168] White, Charles. *Life and Times of Little Richard, Quasar of Rock*. pg. 228

[169] Whiteside, Jonny. *Lee Angel: The Muse Who Had A Front-Row Seat To Rock History*. LA Weekly, May 31, 2018

[170] Ibid.

[171] Himes, Geoffrey, *It's Still Rock 'n' Roll for Little Richard*. Washington Post, May 28, 1999

[172] Grimes, A.C. *The Untold Truth of Little Richard*. www.grunge.com/ 93930/untold-truth-little-richard/

Index

About the Author

TINA ANDREWS is the international award-winning author, screenwriter and playwright who won the Writers Guild of America Award, an NAACP Image Award, and the MIB Prism Award for her 4-hour mega-hit CBS miniseries, *Sally Hemings An American Scandal.* She won an NAACP Image Award, and the Memphis Writers Conference Award for her bestselling nonfiction book, *Sally Hemings An American Scandal: The Struggle To Tell The Controversial True Story.* She is also author of the novels *Charlotte Sophia: Myth, Madness and the Moor;* and *Princess Sarah: Queen Victoria's African Goddaughter.*

Andrews also wrote the screenplay for the Warner Bros. film *Why Do Fools Fall In Love,* the CBS miniseries *"Jacqueline Bouvier Kennedy Onassis,"* and the Showtime animated series, *"Sistas 'n the City."*

Miss Andrews divides her time between New York City and Los Angeles.

Printed in Great Britain
by Amazon